DATE DUE

ILL 11-5-89	
APR 3 0 1992	
ILL 1-11-93	
ILL - 7-12-93 4759770	
ILL 8-10-93	
ILL 9-8-94	
ILL 3-6-95	

BRODART, INC.   Cat. No. 23-221

The Collector's Encyclopedia of
Hall China

Margaret & Kenn Whitmyer

COLLECTOR BOOKS

A Division of Schroeder Publishing Co., Inc.

The current values in this book should be used only as a guide. They are not intended to set prices, which vary from one section of the country to another. Auction prices as well as dealer prices vary greatly and are affected by condition as well as demand. Neither the Author nor the Publisher assumes responsibility for any losses that might be incurred as a result of consulting this guide.

Dedication

This book is dedicated to Dan Tucker and Lorrie Kitchen who have the fatal "Hall China Collection Syndrome." Harmless to humans, but deadly for the pocketbook; the collecting is fun. They invite you to join them.

Acknowledgments

The Collector's Encyclopedia of Hall China has been made possible through the efforts of many faithful collectors and dealers who have been willing to share their knowledge and information with us. We want to thank all of our readers who have sent us pictures and other information which has helped to verify the existence of the many new pieces listed in this book. Due to the volume of mail, we have not been able to respond personally to all of your letters, but we have tried to answer as many as possible. We apologize if you have written to us and have not received an answer. However, we want you to know your letter has been read and the information or suggestions in it have been appreciated.

We appreciate the kindness of Dan Tucker and Lorrie Kitchen who have again provided us with the opportunity to photograph much of the rare Hall China they have acquired over the last few years. They have allowed us to borrow anything and have never questioned its safety or even hinted that maybe we had kept something long enough, that we might be trying to forget where it came from.

Several people again opened up their homes and allowed us to invade their privacy for our seemingly unending photography sessions. The contributions of Pansy and Billie Ramsey, Woody Griffith, Jerry Macke and Linda and Elvin Heck were especially appreciated.

We are also very grateful to the following people who either helped with pricing or supplied us with much needed information: Ken and Carol Baker, Ronald Binkley, Joyce and Parke Bloyer, Don and Irma Brewer, Bob Brushaber, Sam and Becky Collings, Jim and Betty Cooper, Don and Sally Davis, Don and Joyce DeJong, Krystol Ellis, Gene Florence, Leonard and Shirley Graff, Joyce Guilmire, Jerry Harris, Mr. and Mrs. Johnson, Harriet Kurshadt, Pat Kurz, Mr. and Mrs. Joseph Lockard, Merle and Dee Long, Robert and Bernadette Ludwig, Nancy Maben, Jerry and Connie Monarch, Mrs. W.H. Morgan, Benjamin Moulton, Naomi's Antiques To Go, Tom and Jean Niner, Eugene and Jewel Payton, Bill and Sharon Phillips, Mr. and Mrs. Charles Reed, Bonnie Scherrer, Millie Smith, Sue Switzer, Lee Wagner and Delmar and Mary Lou Youngen.

Perhaps one of the hardest working and least recognized persons on a book of this type is the photographer. He's the silent one behind the camera, upon whom the outcome of the entire project depends. Our photographer, Siegfried Kurz, had the patience to endure the seemingly unending and often unorganized sessions, and the ability provide us with outstanding results. For this we are grateful.

Hopefully, we have included everyone, but if someone's name has mysteriously been lost in our mountain of papers, please understand that we are not unappreciative of your co-operation. We do try to keep track of where the information is coming from, but sometimes finding names at the moment you need them is a problem.

Contents

Part II: Kitchenware

Kitchenware Patterns

Part III: Refrigerator Ware

Part IV: Teapots and Coffee Pots

Part V: Other Hall Products

Foreword

The purpose of this book is to provide collectors with a usable guide to the most popularly collected items produced by the Hall China Company of East Liverpool, Ohio. The greatest emphasis will be placed upon the most collectible patterns, but many of the more obscure pieces will be identified and examined. Currently, the greatest collector interest in the production of the Hall China Company lies in the pieces produced between the early 1930's and the late 1950's. We have tried to illustrate and identify as many items from this period as possible.

In the three years since the introduction of our first book, many new discoveries have been unearthed. We appreciate the efforts of the numerous collectors who have taken the time to share their discoveries and collections with us. Much of the new information in this book is a direct result of the efforts of these collectors who have been willing to share their knowledge with us.

Many of the articles from Hall's institutional line have not been included in this guide since there is still little collector interest in most of these items. Some people, who like the superior durability of the ware, are currently buying some of these institutional pieces to use in their kitchens, but most of these items have very little collectible value. The possible exception is the very large black tea servers which may be seen in some fast food chains and restaurants. Older ones, especially those embossed with unusual advertising, are finding homes with collectors.

Many metal, glass and wooden items which match Hall patterns, but were not produced by the company, are also included in this guide. A great number of collectors are now incorporating these matching accessory pieces into their collections.

To provide a more convenient reference, Hall collectibles have been divided into several major categories. Arrangement of patterns and items in each area is essentially alphabetical. The major divisions are as follows:

1. Dinnerware Patterns.
    A. Styles C, D and ruffled -D dinnerware arranged alphabetically.
    B. E-shape dinnerware.
    C. Century shape dinnerware.
    D. Tomorrow's Classic shape dinnerware.
2. Kitchenware.
    A. Basic kitchenware shapes.
    B. Kitchenware patterns.
3. Refrigerator Ware.
4. Teapots and Coffee Pots.
5. Advertising and Specialty Items.

To properly identify a piece of Hall China, more than one name is often necessary. Most items, especially if they have a decal, will have a pattern name, such as Autumn Leaf or Red Poppy. In addition to the pattern name, individual pieces in a pattern will also usually have a shape name. The shape name helps to distinguish like items in the same pattern from each other. For example, if someone tells you they have a teapot in the pattern Red Poppy, you still don't know exactly what they have since there are two different teapots in this pattern. Therefore, the shape name – Aladdin or New York – is used to distinguish between the two similar items in the same pattern. The items in the pictures will be identified by using the name of the pattern where necessary (when more than one pattern is shown in a single photo). This will be followed by the identifying name of the piece, followed by the shape name or color name. Examples are the following:

1. More than one pattern per photo: Acacia (pattern name); jug (item name); "Radiance" (shape name).
2. One pattern per photo: Jug (item name); "Radiance" (shape name).
3. Kitchenware shapes: Teapot (item name); Chinese red (color name).
4. Teapot section: Aladdin (shape name); green (color name).

A lot of the names for the colors, patterns and shapes used in this book are the ones designated by Hall China. However, Hall did not have names for every piece they made. In the event an official Hall name could not be determined for an item, we have taken the liberty of providing one of our own. These new names we have used will be found in quotation marks. Also, over the years, other names have been introduced and accepted by collectors for the identification of some pieces. We have attempted to use those names in this book wherever possible. In some cases certain pieces have evolved with a dual identity. Therefore, a cross reference of multiple names has been included to aid collectors in their attempts to use other references.

Pricing

The prices in this book represent retail prices for mint condition pieces. Items which are excessively worn or chipped or cracked will only bring a fraction of the listed price. A price range has been included to help account for regional differences in prices. Also, be aware that certain currently rare items which are now valued at several hundred dollars, may prove hard to sell if a quantity of these items is discovered. The value of a few items, which are currently one-of-a-kind, may be omitted from the price guide if a retail value has not been established. In these cases the letters "UND." for undetermined will be used to indicate an unestablished value.

All items are priced each, including shakers. Items which have lids are priced complete. Any exceptions to this will be noted in the individual listing. Prices of solid color kitchenware items, refrigerator items, teapots and coffee pots may vary considerably according to color. Wherever possible, an attempt has been made to reflect these different valuations. However, any attempt to list and price the dozens of colors in which some of the pieces may be found is impossible in a guide of this type. An effort has been made to give the reader general guidelines about rarity and desirability of various pieces and colors. Thoughtful consideration of these guidelines should produce a qualitative value for most any item.

Pricing information has been obtained from dealer listings, flea market and show observations, trade publications and from collectors. Remember, prices in this guide should only be used as a reference. Prices may vary in the marketplace, and it is not the intention of the authors to establish or control prices.

Re-issues

Hall China introduced a new retail line to buyers at the Housewares Show held in Chicago in March, 1985. The new line is called "Hall American" and is designed for the retail market through gourmet shops and department stores. In addition to some casseroles, bakers, jugs and teapots which were still in production, Hall revived some shapes from its past. The total number of new shapes available ranges to the mid-60's, but a few of these shapes which reflect the past are of particular interest to collectors. Noteworthy are the re-introduction of the Airflow, Rhythm and square T-Ball teapots; the Donut and Streamline jugs; a square-based "Sundial" batter bowl; and the "Nora" and "Hercules" water servers.

Generally, this line is only available in six standard colors in the retail outlets. The new colors are red, black, white, Sandust (tan), Oxford Grey and Marine Blue. However, any of Hall's colors may be special ordered, and some individual customers have had various pieces introduced in their own unique colors. Therefore, do not be surprised to find new pieces showing up in such colors as lavender, rose or orange.

Fortunately, Hall has considered the concerns of collectors, and all the new production is being marked with the rectangular backstamp which has been in use since 1970.

Colors

Hall produced the widest variety of colored glazes of any china company. Many of the colors are very close, with some only varying by a shade. Due to this small difference, we have tried to reproduce some of the most frequently encountered colors in the accompanying color chart. Even with the help of the chart, it may still be hard to identify some of the colors.

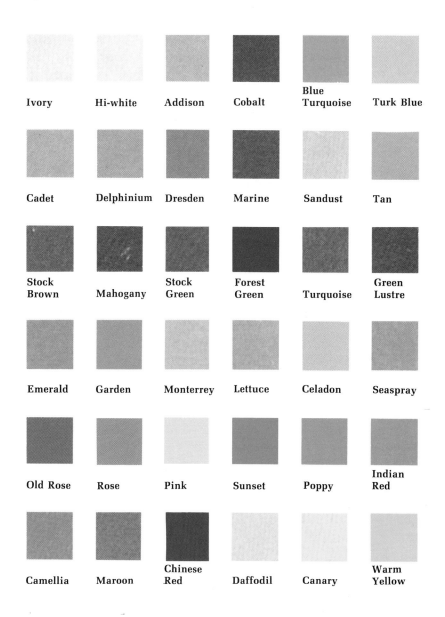

Ivory	Hi-white	Addison	Cobalt	Blue Turquoise	Turk Blue
Cadet	Delphinium	Dresden	Marine	Sandust	Tan
Stock Brown	Mahogany	Stock Green	Forest Green	Turquoise	Green Lustre
Emerald	Garden	Monterrey	Lettuce	Celadon	Seaspray
Old Rose	Rose	Pink	Sunset	Poppy	Indian Red
Camellia	Maroon	Chinese Red	Daffodil	Canary	Warm Yellow

History of the Hall China Company

The Hall China Company was established by Robert Hall on August 14, 1903, as a result of the dissolution of the East Liverpool Potteries Company. The first plant was located in the old West, Hardwick and George building at Fourth and Walnut Streets in East Liverpool, Ohio. Initially, 38 potters were employed at three kilns to produce spittoons and combinets. In 1904, Robert Hall died and his son, Robert Taggert Hall, became manager.

Robert T. Hall kept the plant operating by producing primarily toilet sets, jugs and other white ware. At the same time, he experimented endlessly to re-discover a lost process from the Ming Dynasty (A.D. 1368-1644) in China, which would allow him to produce non-lead glazed china with a single-fire process. This single-firing would allow the glaze to penetrate the unfired body, creating a craze-proof finish. Robert T. Hall experimented from 1904 until 1911 before he finally achieved success. His new process created a colorfully glazed china which was strong, non-porous and craze-proof.

Hall China experimented briefly with dinnerware from 1908 until 1911, but then chose to concentrate on institutional wares. As the company grew and the institutional line expanded, two more plants were added in East Liverpool. The successful addition of their Gold Decorated Teapot Line pushed the capacity of these plants to the limit. In 1930, a new plant was built on the east side of East Liverpool, and the three old plants were abandoned. This new plant enjoyed numerous expansions during the 1930's and early 1940's as production boomed with the introduction of decal dinnerware and kitchenware patterns.

The Hall China Company is still operating in this plant today. Once again, production is targeted primarily at institutional and commercial customers. However, Hall has recently re-introduced some of its old kitchenware shapes for the retail trade and is always willing to accomodate the special needs of its customers.

The China Process

The manufacturing of Hall China begins with a secret powdered mixture of flint, feldspar and several different clays. These ingredients are mixed with water in a machine. The resulting slip is passed through separators which remove metals and other foreign objects.

The mixture is then pumped into presses which squeeze out the water, leaving clay in a cake form. The cakes of clay are then aged and pressed through pug mills which remove air from the clay.

The clay is then shaped by a "jiggerman" on a potters' wheel to form flat pieces and bowls. To produce pieces such as teapots or jugs, water is added to the clay, and the resulting slip is poured into a mould. The raw ware is allowed to dry for 24 hours at about 100°F. Then the special leadless glaze is applied by either spraying or hand-dipping. The glazed items are placed on cars which move slowly through a kiln. The temperature of the ware slowly is increased to 2400°F. This intense heat causes chemical changes in the body and glaze materials which allows the color to set.

The fired china is then inspected for defects and the good pieces are sent on to the decorating department. Decorating is done by either hand-painting or by transferring decals or prints to the ware. The finished product is then re-fired in a smaller oven at a lower temperature. Decals were a very popular method of decoration during the 1930's and 1940's. Since only pieces of larger decals were sometimes used on smaller item in a pattern, it is sometimes difficult to associate these pieces with the rest of the items in the pattern. Careful comparison will usually result in a positive identification.

Identification of Hall China

#1

#2

#3

#4

#5

Pictured here are the general backstamps which may be found on the bottom of Hall China. Certain other backstamps which are peculiar to a particular pattern will be found illustrated in the section portraying the individual pattern.

Backstamp #1 is a very early mark. This mark was used until the early teens and will not be found on much "collectible" Hall China. An example of a pitcher with this mark is shown on page 13.

Backstamp #2 was used from the early teens until the late 1920's. Early Gold Decorated Line teapots produced during this period will bear this mark.

Mark #3 is the backstamp which appears most frequently on items of interest to today's collector. This mark was used from the early 1930's until about 1970 and will be found on most items except kitchenware and dinnerware. These two categories have special backstamps.

Mark #4 was used on kitchenware produced after 1932. This mark was usually stamped in gold, but will also be found in black, blue, green and perhaps a few other colors. Occasionally a pattern name will also appear in conjunction with this mark.

Backstamp #5 was reserved for Hall dinnerware. This mark was modified slightly for use with the dinnerware produced for the Jewel Tea Company and for the Orange Poppy and Wildfire patterns of The Great American Tea Company. Autumn Leaf will have "Tested and Approved by MARY DUNBAR--JEWEL HOMEAKERS IN-STITUTE" in the circle. Orange Poppy has the Great American Golden Key symbol inside the circle and the Wildfire mark acknowledges the 100th anniversary of Great American. For examples of these marks, see the dinnerware section.

Fortunately for collectors, most of Hall's items have an identifying backstamp. With the exception of shakers, lamps and some coffee pots, most of the unmarked pieces of Hall were seconds and never reached the decorating room.

In addition to the above printed backstamps, some items will be found with "HALL" impressed in large block letters. Many of the kitchenware pieces with this mark will date to the early 1930's or before. Many institutional pieces will also be marked in this manner.

Paper labels were also used by Hall. However, since most items were used heavily, not much Hall China is found with paper labels still intact. Paper labels are helpful in identifying lamps which Hall made for the White Lamp Company and others. The only way to identify these lamps as Hall is by their paper label since there is no backstamp.

Hall China produced since the early 1970's has the following backstamp:

Early Hall

Although examples are scarce today, some highly collectible pieces of Hall China were made during the early years. The two items shown here were made in the early 1900's.

The larger pitcher on the right is 7½″ tall and was produced by the East Liverpool Potteries Company. The backstamp (shown to the right) on this pitcher was used prior to August, 1903, when the principals, which included Robert Hall, chose to dissolve the company. Robert Hall took over one of the abandoned buildings and formed the Hall China Company.

The smaller pitcher is 6¾″ tall and bears the #1 Hall backstamp.

Backstamp of
East Liverpool Potteries Company.

Part I: Dinnerware

Row 1: C-style; D-style; Ruffled D-style. **Row 2:** E-style; Century style; Tomorrow's Classic style.

Hall began producing decal pattern dinnerware in 1936 with the introduction of an Autumn Leaf breakfast set. During the next 20 years many different patterns and several different shapes of dinnerware were produced. The dinnerware patterns and shapes will be identified and evaluated in this section. Styles of dinnerware found in this guide include:

D-style. This was the most commonly used shape of dinnerware. The plates and bowls are round and the cups and gravy boat have ear-shaped handles. Although there are some minor modifications in the different patterns, the basic dinnerware service consists of the following pieces:

Bowl, 5¼″ fruit	Cup	Plate, 9″
Bowl, 6″ cereal	Gravy Boat	Platter, 11¼″ oval
Bowl, 8½″ flat soup	Plate, 6″	Platter, 13¼″ oval
Bowl, 9″ vegetable	Plate, 8″	Saucer

C-style. The C-style pieces have the same round shape as the D-style. However, all the C-style dinnerware is embossed with the "Radiance" design. The cup does not have an ear-shaped handle and there is no gravy boat. The only pattern which has been found with this shape dinnerware is Orange Poppy.

Ruffled D-style. This is a modified D-style. The flat pieces and the bowls have a scalloped edge instead of just being plain round. Two additional sizes of plates – a 10″ dinner and a 7¼″ salad – were also included in the set. This shape is exclusive to the Autumn Leaf pattern.

E-style. The E-style dinnerware shape was designed by J. Palin Thorley and was produced during the 1940's and early 1950's. Many of the patterns which use this shape were produced for Sears, but several non-Sears products were also made.

Century shape. The Century shape was designed in the 1950's by Eva Zeisel. The shape of the plates is slightly oval with a prominent tab handle. Bowls and platters have two distinct tab handles.

Tomorrow's Classic shape. Tomorrow's Classic is another shaped designed by Eva Zeisel in the 1950's. It is similar in style to the Century shape. However, the plates are slightly oval and lack a tab handle, and the bowls and platters feature a single tab handle. There are other minor differences among the other serving pieces in the two shapes, but the butter dish and the gravy boat are the same shape in both lines.

Arrangement of the dinnerware patterns in this chapter is alphabetical in three separate sections. The first section includes a combined listing of all C, D and Ruffled-D shape dinnerware. This is followed by an alphabetical listing of the E-style dinnerware. The final section presents a listing of the Century and Tomorrow's Classic shapes designed by Eva Zeisel.

As with many other popular collectibles, there are numerous items resembling Autumn Leaf pieces which have been fashioned by ingenious individuals. In many cases, these attempts at imitating or adding to the original collectible have served a useful purpose, and there has been no attempt by the maker to defraud the public or misrepresent the article. However, the problem with these articles occurs when they reach the secondary market where people are unfamiliar with their origin. Novice collectors who find any unusual china piece, especially if it lacks the Jewel backstamp or shows few signs of age, would be well advised to check the authenticity of the piece with another knowledgeable collector or dealer before paying a high price for such an item. Some of the homemade non-china items are showing up at flea markets, and collectors should be aware that these are recent creations which should not command the exhorbitant prices reserved for truly rare items. The following is a list of creations which we have been able to compile and their original prices where they were available:

Item	Original Price
Clock made from a 10″ dinner plate	65.00
Ceramic two-part reamer	25.00
Ceramic square hotplate	
Ceramic tureen/underplate/ladle	38.50
Ceramic dinner bell on a wooden rack	19.50
Ceramic butter with dome shape ceramic lid	
Ceramic dresser box	
Ceramic large turkey platter	38.50
Ceramic wall switch and outlet plates	8.50
Ceramic footed candy dish	25.50
Ceramic egg cup	10.50
Ceramic soap dish	7.00
Ceramic toothpick holder	5.00
Ceramic pie lifter	7.00

Item	Original Price
Ceramic spoon rest	7.00
Ceramic napkin holder	10.00
Ceramic tissue box	25.00
Ceramic square ruffled candy and cover	25.00
Ceramic child's set, four place setting	100.00
Ceramic lamp	100.00
Handmade quilt	
Glass cheese dome/wooden base and inlaid tile	38.50
Tall wooden hand-painted salt/pepper	
Six peg oak coat rack	28.50
Oak paper towel holder	38.50
Wooden cutting board	
Metal match safe	
Small one- and two-cup metal sifters	

In addition to the above there are also reports of the existence of several hand-painted kitchen chairs.

Japanese canister and condiment set with decal similar to Autumn Leaf.

Non-Hall china with an Autumn Leaf decal made by American Limoges.

Collectors who are interested in Autumn Leaf should consider becoming members of the National Autumn Leaf Collectors Club. Besides meeting and becoming friends with other members who are interested in the same collectible, other benefits include the opportunity to keep up with new developments and the ability to buy, sell and trade extra pieces. The club has also commissioned Hall to produce a special New York teapot and an Edgewater vase for its members. These items, which are pictured here, have a backstamp which identifies them as being made exclusively for the club. For membership information contact the National Autumn Leaf Collectors Club, C/o Artie Arce, 8813 Collingwood, Austin, TX 78748.

New York teapot made for The National Autumn Leaf Collectors Club in 1984.

Edgewater vase made for the National Autumn Leaf Collectors Club in 1987.

Autumn Leaf Dinnerware

Abundant supplies of reasonably priced Autumn Leaf basic dinnerware pieces have enticed many people to begin collecting this pattern. Many collections have blossomed from the cheap acquisition of a few pieces at a garage sale, flea market or auction. Other collectors have gotten their starts through the inheritance of a few pieces from a close relative. Natural curiosity and the thirst for knowledge have driven them to pursue the elusive Autumn Leaf motif. How many of them would have begun if they had realized the vast number of accessory pieces available and the enormous sums of money required to acquire them?

Most dinnerware articles were made for a long period of time—from the 1930's and 1940's until the mid-1970's. Therefore, many of these items are readily available at a moderate price and collectors should expect to be able to purchase pieces which are in excellent condition. The only dinnerware pieces which appear to be in short supply are the cream soups and the 10″ plates. Even these can be found by most collectors without extreme effort.

Although the crazing problem with this china is minimal, extensive use will result in abnormal wear and damage to the gold rim. Dinnerware which is scratched or dull will only bring a fraction of the listed prices. Some collectors, who want to use their china, buy these slightly worn pieces to use for everyday in order to preserve the value of the pieces in their collections.

Although Autumn Leaf kitchenware was made earlier, the first dinnerware appeared in 1936. Jewel ads of the time promoted this as the first dinnerware ever produced by Hall China and expounded on its beauty and durability. The new dishes were "manufactured from the best imported and domestic clays. The china has been tested for an hour under 100 pounds of pressure at a temperature of 212° and then doused with cold water. No cracks or crazes developed." The initial offering consisted of a 24-piece set which included four of each of the following: 9″ breakfast plates, 5½″ deep fruit bowls, cups and saucers. The complete set sold for $4.95.

Two sizes of oval platters were added to the dinnerware line in 1938. The 11″ platter sold for 65¢ and the 13″ platter was listed at $1.00.

The small 7 ounce custard cup shown on the right side of the bottom row was one of numerous items added to the Autumn Leaf line in 1936. This was Jewel's Item No. 303 and was sold as a set of six for $1.00.

		Item	Introduced	Discontinued	Price
Top Photo	Row 1:	Plate, 10″	1938	1976*	8.00-10.00
		Plate, 9″	1936	1976	4.00-5.00
		Plate, 8″	1938	1976	6.00-8.00
	Row 2:	Plate 7¼″	1938	1976	4.00-5.00
		Plate, 6″	1938	1976	2.50-3.50
		Platter, 9″ oval	1942	1976	12.00-15.00
	Row 3:	Platter, 11½″ oval	1938	1976	10.00-12.00
		Platter, 13½″ oval	1938	1976*	12.00-14.00
Bottom Photo	Row 1:	Bowl, 8½″ flat soup	1938	1976*	8.00-10.00
		Bowl, 6½″ cereal	1938	1976	6.00-8.00
		Bowl, 5½″ fruit	1936	1976*	3.00-4.00
		Custard, "Radiance"	1936	1976	3.00-4.00

*Re-issued later (1978)

Autumn Leaf Cups, Bowls, Sugars & Creamers

The difference between the "old style" and "new style" sugar and creamer is shown in the top row. The older style sugar and creamer first appeared with the No. 300 coffee service in 1936. The handles and the vertical rays match the shape and style of the other kitchenware pieces from this period. The newer sugar and creamer was introduced in 1940. The shape of the handles on this set matches the shape of the handles on the dinnerware pieces. The "Rayed" set was made for a much shorter period and is harder to find than the ruffled-D set. Significant differences also exist between the two styles of sugar lids. The old style lid is flatter and has a "bud" knob with rays. The newer lid is more sloped and has a "bud" knob which lacks rays. Beware of buying lids which have had their knobs glued back on.

The second row pictures the mugs, cups and saucers available in the Autumn Leaf pattern. The first cup and saucer shown is the regular dinnerware style. This set was called the "breakfast cup and saucer" in Jewel ads. The larger cup and saucer represents a style referred to as St. Denis. This cup and saucer is sometimes called the "he man" style. It was introduced in 1942, and the original price was 45¢ for a cup and saucer. By the time these pieces were discontinued in 1976, the price of the cup had increased to $2.50 and the saucer was listed at $1.25.

The "conic" mug was listed in Jewel catalogs as a 10 oz. beverage mug. The introductory price was $6.95 for a set of four in 1966. This same 1966 catalog also heralded the introduction of the Irish coffee mugs which "lets you serve coffee in a new and different way . . . eliminates use of saucers." The original price of these mugs was $7.95 for a set of four. When they were discontinued in 1976, beverage mugs were selling for $22.00 for a set of four and four Irish coffee mugs cost $27.00 in 1976. The Irish coffee mugs, which are now selling for more than 10 times their last cost through Jewel, have appreciated considerably since they were discontinued.

The two-quart salad bowl is shown in the left side of the third shelf. It was introduced in 1937 as Jewel's Item No. 312, and cost 95¢. When the bowl was discontinued in 1976, it cost $4.95. The long run of this bowl has produced a bountiful supply, thus, the current price is moderate.

The salad fork with the Autumn Leaf decal is very rare. The quality of this piece suggests it may have been made by Hall for Jewel. However, it appears to have been a sample item. So few have been found that there are doubts that it was ever offered for sale.

The round 9″ vegetable bowl appears on the right side of the third shelf. This bowl was only made for a few years, between 1937 and 1939. Therefore, it is rather difficult to find and has become expensive.

The two styles of oval bowls are shown on the bottom row. The bowl on the left is divided and is much harder to find than the undivided style. The divided bowl was designed to serve two vegetables in the same bowl and was available from 1957 through 1976. In 1976, the oval bowl sold for $7.95, and the divided bowl sold for $10.95. Today, the value of the oval bowl has about doubled, but the value of the divided bowl has increased more than five-fold.

		Item	Introduced	Discontinued	Price
Top Photo	Row 1:	Sugar and lid, "Rayed"	1934	1940	12.00-15.00
		Creamer, "Rayed"	1934	1940	10.00-12.00
		Sugar and lid, ruffled-D	1940	1976	9.00-11.00
		Creamer, ruffled-D	1934	1940	6.00-8.00
	Row 2:	Cup, ruffled-D	1936	1976	4.00-5.00
		Saucer, ruffled-D	1936	1976	1.00-1.50
		Cup, St. Denis	1942		12.00-14.00
		Saucer, St. Denis	1942		4.00-5.00
		Mug, conic	1966	1976*	30.00-35.00
		Mug, Irish coffee	1966	1976*	60.00-75.00
Bottom Photo	Row 1:	Bowl, salad	1937	1976	10.00-12.00
		Fork, salad			300.00-350.00
		Bowl, 9″ round	1937	1939	50.00-60.00
	Row 2:	Bowl, oval divided	1957	1976	45.00-50.00
		Bowl, oval	1939	1976*	12.00-15.00

*Re-issued later (1978)

Autumn Leaf Condiments, Warmers & Accessories

Even though cake lifters are not generally attributed to Hall, the Autumn Leaf example pictured in the top row is generally accepted as a Hall product. Although quite a few of the more advanced collectors own one, cake lifters with the Autumn Leaf decal were not available through regular Jewel catalogs, and collectors who are still searching will find them very difficult to locate.

The round 9½″ cake plate is one of the most commonly found pieces of Autumn Leaf. The cake plate was added to the line in 1937 and was discontinued in 1976. This was a truly multi-purpose item and was priced at 75¢ in 1937. It was designed to fit perfectly into the previously introduced metal cake carriers and could also be used as a serving plate or as a tile under the casseroles or coffee servers. In addition, the two raised rings on the underside allowed it to become a cover for the utility bowls.

The small two handle round bowl on the right side of the top row is a cream soup. It is shown here sitting on the breakfast cup saucer which is often used as an underplate for this piece.

The oval covered vegetable dish shown on the second row was introduced in 1940 and discontinued in 1976. Jewel's price for this piece in 1949 was $2.75. As with many other Jewel items, replacement of a damaged part was simple since the top and the bottom could be purchased separately.

The gravy boat was also introduced in 1940 and was discontinued in 1976. It is shown here sitting on the 8½″ oval pickle dish which also doubles as the underplate for the gravy boat. The oval pickle was added to the line in 1942. In 1949, the gravy boat was priced at $1.25 and the cost of the pickle dish was 75¢.

The first warmer shown is not actually Autumn Leaf since it lacks the decal. However, the attractive gold decoration on this piece makes it very desirable as a go-along item. The oval warmer in the center was designed for use with the Aladdin shape teapot. The round warmer shown on the right was used with the coffee servers or the round casserole. Both shapes contain a built-in candleholder in the center and came boxed with four candles. The selling price of both warmers in 1960, the year they were discontinued, was $2.25.

Three different style condiment jars are pictured on the bottom row. In answer to a lot of questions, no china spoons were provided for these jars by either Jewel or Hall. The larger jar on the left side is a marmalade, and the one in the center is a mustard. Both these items made their appearance in 1938 and disappeared the following year. Even though both were only produced for a short time, collectors seem to have only moderate difficulty in obtaining them. Notice the underplates are different sizes. The diameter of the marmalade underplate is 6″, and the diameter of the mustard underplate is 4¾″. The 3½″ tall condiment jar on the right is not commonly found. Very little is known about this jar and it is believed to have been submitted by Hall in about 1941 as a sample item. Jewel must have rejected this design, and since it was never put into regular production, few collectors will ever experience the joy of owning one.

		Item	Introduced	Discontinued	Price
Top Photo	Row 1:	Cake server			175.00-200.00
		Cake plate	1937	1976	10.00-12.00
		Cream soup	1950	1976	15.00-18.00
	Row 2:	Dish, oval covered	1940	1976	28.00-32.00
		Gravy boat	1940	1976	18.00-20.00
		Gravy boat underplate	1942	1976	10.00-14.00
Bottom Photo	Row 1:	Warmer, no decal			20.00-25.00
		Warmer, oval	1955	1960	90.00-110.00
		Warmer, round	1956	1960	75.00-90.00
	Row 2:	Condiment, marmalade	1938	1939	42.00-47.00
		Condiment, mustard	1938	1939	35.00-38.00
		Condiment, experimental			400.00-450.00

Autumn Leaf Kitchenware

Two styles of Autumn Leaf bean pots are pictured on the top shelf—one handle and two handle. Of the two, the one handle variety is much harder to find. The two handle version was re-issued in 1978. There are slight differences between the two issues. The major difference is in the gold decoration on top of the handles. The older one has three gold lines, and the newer one has a single gold stripe on the handle. Although the lids for both the one handle and two handle bean pots are the same size, they are not interchangeable. The lid to the two handle pot simply has a gold band around the knob, while the lid to the other one has the gold band plus an Autumn Leaf flower in the center of the knob.

Three different sizes of fluted bakers are shown on the second row. The largest holds three pints and sold for 85¢ in 1939. The one in the middle holds two pints and the smallest one holds 10 ounces. The two-pint fluted baker is not easy to find, and the price of this size baker is rising steadily. The small baker is commonly found and was re-issued in 1978. The re-issued baker is about ¼″ larger than the original baker.

The covered family casserole was introduced as a special premium for Jewel's 36th anniversary in 1935. The price of this item in 1939 was $1.75. The pie baker, which is shown in the center of row three, bakes a 9½″ pie and was guaranteed to heat evenly. This resulted in a perfectly baked pie with "no burnt crusts." The shallow oval bowl on the right side of the third row holds 12 ounces and is often called a Fort Pitt oval baker. It was a convenient item since it held individual size portions and allowed the food to be baked and served in the same dish.

The oval baker pictured below is similar in shape to the Fort Pitt baker, but it is larger. This baker holds two pints and measures 10″ long by 7½″ wide by 2¼″ deep. At the present time, only a few of these have been found.

The three-piece utility bowl set was introduced in 1939. If the number available today is any indication, this must have been one of Jewel's more successful offerings. The set cost $2.65 when it was introduced and had only increased to $4.95 by 1960. The three-piece set consists of a large 3½ quart bowl, a medium-sized two quart bowl and a small one quart bowl. They were advertised as being ideal for mixing, baking, serving and storing.

	Item	Introduced	Discontinued	Price
Row 1:	Bean pot, 1-handle, 2¼ qt.			200.00-235.00
	Bean pot, 2-handle	1960	1976*	70.00-90.00
Row 2:	Baker, French, 3 pt.	1936	1976	10.00-12.00
	Baker, French, 2 pt.	1966	1976	28.00-32.00
	Baker, French, 4¾″	1978	1978*	12.00-15.00
	Baker, French, 4½″	1966	1976	5.00-7.00
Row 3:	Casserole, round 2 qt.	1935	1976	18.00-22.00
	Pie baker	1937	1976	15.00-18.00
	Baker, Fort Pitt, 12 oz.	1966	1976	50.00-60.00
Row 4:	Bowl, 9″ "Radiance"	1933	1976	12.00-14.00
	Bowl, 7½″ "Radiance"	1933	1976	10.00-12.00
	Bowl, 6″ "Radiance"	1933	1976	9.00-10.00

*Re-issued 1978

Rare 10″ Autumn Leaf oval baker.

Autumn Leaf Kitchenware

The modern-style cookie jar with the two big ear-like handles was added to the Autumn Leaf line in 1957. Jewel liked to call these handles "easy-grip" and sold the cookie jar for $3.00. The shape of the jar came from a line designed by Eva Zeisel, and many collectors call this style "Zeisel" to distinguish this cookie from the earlier shape cookie jar which is shown in the center of the top row.

The old style cookie jar was introduced for Christmas 1936. It was a dual purpose item since it could also be used as a bean pot. This cookie jar sold for $1.50 and was only offered for three years.

The Autumn Leaf four-piece stack set is pictured on the right side of the top row. It consists of three separate stacking containers and one lid. Each of the stacking units is a different size. The bottom one holds 34 ounces; the center one holds 24 ounces; and the top one holds 18 ounces. The complete set sold for $5.25 in 1960.

The ball-shaped beverage jug was an outstanding success for Jewel. This may be seen by the availability of this item today at shows and flea markets. It has a 5½ pint capacity and was designed with an ice lip to trap ice cubes while pouring.

An Autumn Leaf batter jug is shown in the center of the second row. Not much is known about when this piece was made. It may have been a special promotion since it is quite rare to find one today.

The 2½ pint utility pitcher was introduced in 1937. It was a multi-purpose kitchen item which was convenient for either beverages or batter.

Tidbit trays made an appearance in 1954. These trays were made from plates in the regular dinnerware line. However, plates which were selected for use in the trays do not have a backstamp in the normal position. The large 10¼" plates have an off-center backstamp so the holes for the center handle were not drilled through the backstamp. Also, the smaller plates which are used in the tidbit have no backstamp. The three-tiered tidbit offered in the 1960 catalog sold for $4.00. At various times a two-tiered tidbit was also available.

	Item	Introduced	Discontinued	Price
Row 1:	Cookie jar, Zeisel	1957	1969	70.00-80.00
	Cookie jar, "Rayed"	1936	1939	80.00-90.00
	Stack set	1951	1976	50.00-55.00
Row 2:	Ball jug #3	1938	1976	18.00-20.00
	Batter jug, "Sundial"			800.00-1,000.00
	Jug, 2½ pt. "Rayed"	1937	1976	11.00-13.00
Row 3:	Tidbit, 3-tier	1954	1969	35.00-40.00
	Tidbit, 2-tier	1954	1969	30.00-35.00

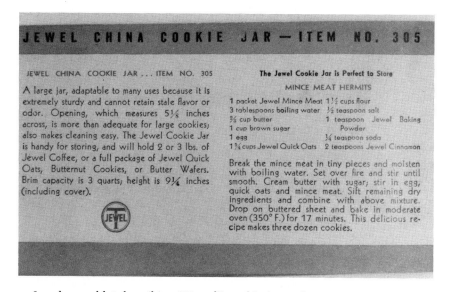

Jewel pamphlet describing "Rayed" cookie jar and suggesting a recipe.

Autumn Leaf Coffee Pots and Teapots

The first Autumn Leaf coffee pot appeared in 1934. It was a nine-cup server and was introduced as part of a complete coffee service set which also included the oval 18¾″ metal tray, an asbestos hot pad and the old style sugar and creamer. The price of the complete set was $5.25 in 1937. The coffee server came with a metal dripper which was made by the West Bend Aluminum Company. This dripper had also been used on previous Jewel all-metal coffee pots. The nine-cup server remained in the line until 1942.

In November 1936, Jewel added another coffee server to the Autumn Leaf line. This was an eight-cup maker and was lauded in their ads as being "improved for the making of perfect coffee and modernized in appearance." The lid of this pot would not fit the metal dripper. The new dripper was designed to "aid in the flow of water and to simplify coffee making." Apparently this new concept was short-lived. Ads for the eight-cup coffee server from late 1937 indicate the dripper was redesigned. The new dripper had the Autumn Leaf motif and was made so the cover of the coffee server also fit the dripper. On occasion, glass drippers will be found with some coffee servers. The war-time restrictions during World War II necessitated this alteration. In later years, the eight-cup coffee pot came complete with a measuring spoon and an asbestos pad. This style set sold for $6.25 in the 1960 Jewel catalog.

The introduction of another coffee maker was also prompted by war-time restrictions. The five-cup all-china coffee maker made an appearance in 1942. The new design was implemented to meet the government's request to conserve coffee and also eliminated the need for the use of any metal in its manufacture. According to the ads, the china dripper conserved coffee since it was designed "to bring out the maximum flavor so less than the usual amount of coffee is needed to brew a cup of normal strength."

The ultimate in automation in coffee brewing was achieved in 1957 when the automatic electric percolator was added to the line. It featured a safety-lock top, switched automatically to warming heat after brewing, and was guaranteed for a full year against any defects in workmanship. The retail price of this marvel was only $19.95.

Teapots played an important role in the early development of the Autumn Leaf line. The first teapot, the Newport shape, was introduced in 1933. It was a square seven-cup teapot which sold for $1.50. Two years later, it was replaced by a combination tea/coffee pot. This was the familiar long-spout pot which could be used to make either seven cups of tea or four cups of coffee. A small metal dripper was provided to institute the conversion from a teapot to a coffee pot. This new pot was also priced at $1.50.

The Newport teapot was reissued in 1978. There are several differences between the old version and the newer one. The old teapot has no gold around the tip of the spout and the decal is larger than the decal on the later teapot. The teapot from 1978 has gold around the tip of the spout and has a decal with a pink leaf. The two lids are also different. The hole in the older lid is to the side of the knob while the hole in the newer lid is in front of the knob. The advent of the seven-cup Aladdin teapot in 1942 with the china tea strainer eliminated the need for the metal tea ball. Judging from the number of Aladdins seen today, the success of this teapot must have been phenomenal. Autumn Leaf purists collect two different versions of this teapot – long spout and short spout. The difference here was probably not intentional. Instead, the variation appears to be the result of slight mould variations. The Aladdin teapot was listed in a 1960 catalog for $4.25.

	Item	Introduced	Discontinued	Price
Row 1:	Coffee pot, 9-cup "Rayed"	1934	1941	30.00-35.00
	Coffee pot, 8-cup "Rayed"/open drip (not shown)	1936	1937	28.00-32.00
	Coffee pot, 8-cup "Rayed"	1937	1976	25.00-30.00
Row 2:	Electric Percolator	1957	1969	200.00-250.00
	Drip coffee, all-china	1942	1945	170.00-190.00
	Teapot, "Rayed"	1935	1942	35.00-45.00
Row 3:	Teapot, 1930's Newport	1933	1935	90.00-110.00
	Teapot, 1970's Newport	1978	1978	75.00-85.00
	Teapot, Aladdin	1942	1976	30.00-35.00

Autumn Leaf Accessories

A few of the pieces pictured on the opposite page are among the scarcest in the Autumn Leaf pattern. The "Medallion" style shakers shown on the top row are the only ones that have been found at this writing. The sugar and tea canisters have now been joined by a coffee canister. If anyone can offer any assistance in finding the fourth canister to complete the canister set, I'm sure they would make the owner of these three lonely canisters very happy. The same person would also like to find the mate to the single candle shown in the bottom right corner. These sample items came from former employees who got them from Jewel's employee store. Is it possible that another employee might have gotten other similar samples that are still to be unearthed?

The ruffled base shakers were designed to be used with the Autumn Leaf dinnerware service. According to sources at Hall, the small-size version was introduced first. However, these were too small to be practical, and they were soon replaced with the larger size shakers. The first pair of ruffled base shakers shown on the second row is the normal-size pair. They were first offered in 1939 and were priced at four pairs for $1.00. The pair shown next to them is smaller – just 2″ high – and only a few pair of this size have been found.

The handled shakers and drip jar comprise the range

set which was introduced in 1936. The price of the complete set in 1939 was $1.50. Many of the drip jars were used for other purposes, such as soup bowls or lidless butters. Therefore, a surplus of bottoms exists today.

A clock, which was made from the cake plate mold, was released in 1956. A Master Crafters movement was inserted into a large hole in the center of the cakeplate. A clock which still has its original movement will have the name "HALL" stamped on its face. Clocks could be hung on the wall or set upright on a shelf with the use of an attached wire stand. The clock shown on the left is the style which is normally found. The other clock, with the exposed hands, is quite rare since it was not released for sale. It was a "sales award" item shich was reserved for Jewel salesmen.

So few of the morning tea sets, shown on the bottom shelf, have been found that it can be assumed they were never a regular production item. This set is the same style as other morning sets which were made in some of Hall's kitchenware patterns. The teapot is identical to the teapot used in the No. 1 tea set. However the sugar and creamer were restyled and feature the addition of handles. Also added was a lid for the sugar which matches the style of the teapot lid.

		Item	Introduced	Discontinued	Price
Top Photo	Row 1:	Canister			500.00-600.00
		Shaker, "Medallion"			175.00-200.00
	Row 2:	Shaker, regular size ruffled, ea.	1939	1976	6.00-7.00
		Shaker, miniature ruffled, ea.	1939	1939	125.00-150.00
		Shaker, range, ea.	1936	1976	7.00-8.00
		Drip jar	1936	1976	10.00-12.00
Bottom Photo	Row 1:	Clock	1956	1959	250.00-275.00
		Clock, "salesman's award"	1980	1980	150.00-200.00
	Row 2:	Sugar & lid, morning			90.00-100.00
		Teapot, morning			400.00-500.00
		Creamer, morning			80.00-90.00
		Candleholder, 4″			400.00-475.00

Autumn Leaf Butters, Vases & Accessories

Two sizes of butter dishes were made for Jewel by Hall – one pound and one-quarter pound. As may be seen from the photo, there are several different styles of each size butter. A quick glance at the prices indicates none of these butters is common. However, one style in each size will be obtainable for the average collector with a little diligent searching.

The first butter dish listed in the Jewel catalogs was the one-pound dish shown in the center of the second row. It was introduced in 1959 and sold for $3.25. Its design proved to be inconvenient, and this butter was discontinued after only one season. This style of pound butter was in very short supply until a quantity of unsold ones was discovered in a warehouse in the early 1980's. This find has been slowly absorbed by collectors, and the price of this butter has been steadily rising as its availability decreases.

The other two one-pound butter dishes are probably experimental designs submitted by Hall as improvements to the original version. Both are the same shape as the original, but they have a knob which is easier to grip. The only difference between these two butters is the one on the right has a "bud" knob with rays and the other one on the left has the same style knob without the rays. The lid without the rays is 5/16″ taller than the one with the rays. The underplate for all three styles is the same.

The replacement for the pound butter was introduced in 1961 in the form of the quarter pound butter shown on the left side of the top row. Another variety of quarter pound butter, the wings style, shown in the center of the

top row, was also introduced the same year. Judging from their availability today, this shape must not have been very popular. The other one-quarter pound butter with the smooth top grip is found frequently enough to suggest it was more than a mere sample item. It is possible this may have been a "sales award" item. The underplate for the first and third butters is the same, while the underplate for the "wings" style butter is more deeply curved.

Two varieties of the bud vase are shown. Variations in size and place of application of the decal are common occurences in the Autumn Leaf pattern and these two vases are an excellent example. The more commonly found vase is the one with the larger decal shown on the right.

The two large vases shown on the top row of the bottom picture have no backstamp to indicate they were made by Hall. Nor is there any evidence to associate them with Jewel Tea. However, they are striking examples of pieces with the Autumn Leaf decal and exhibit the same excellent quality in both pottery and glaze which other Hall pieces possess.

The footed cakestand and the footed candy were both introduced in 1959. The metal base could be unscrewed from the china piece and used as a candle holder. Originally, each piece sold for $4.95. Today, the footed cakestand is found much more readily than the footed candy.

The covered candy jar shown in the center of the bottom row is probably an experimental one-of-a-kind piece. Sources indicate it was made by Hall, was submitted to Jewel as a sample, but was never put into production.

		Item	Introduced	Discontinued	Price
Top Photo	Row 1:	Butter, ¼ pound, regular	1961	1976	85.00-100.00
		Butter, ¼ pound, wings	1961		350.00-425.00
		Butter, ¼ pound, smooth top grip			325.00-375.00
	Row 2:	Butter, one pound, "bud" knob			400.00-500.00
		Butter, one pound, regular	1959	1960	135.00-150.00
		Butter, one pound, "bud ray" knob			400.00-500.00
Bottom Photo	Row 1:	Vase, small decal	1940		125.00-150.00
		Vase, regular decal	1940		125.00-150.00
		Vase or lamp base, 11″			400.00-500.00
		Vase, 7¾″			400.00-500.00
	Row 2:	Cakestand, metal base	1958	1969	95.00-110.00
		Candy jar, experimental			700.00-900.00
		Candy, metal base	1958	1969	260.00-300.00

Autumn Leaf Paper & Plastic Articles

Several different styles of hotpads have been found associated with the Autumn Leaf pattern. Some are readily identifiable with the pattern, and some which were supplied with the coffee servers lack the pattern and are not commonly thought of as Autumn Leaf. The black asbestos hotpads shown on the top shelf were supplied with coffee service sets during the 1930's. A cream color cardboard hotpad with a tin back was introduced in 1937. Another type of hotpad with a creamy wax-like coating and a green or red felt backing was introduced later.

Plastic covers for appliances and bowls were introduced in 1950. An eight piece set of bowl covers in assorted sizes with a drawstring plastic holder sold for one dollar in 1950. In 1960, a seven piece set which included a toaster cover and six bowl covers in assorted sizes sold for $.98. These bowl covers ranged in size from 5″ to 13″. Other plastic covers include a Mary Dunbar mixer cover and a standard-size mixer cover.

Two styles of playing cards were introduced in 1943. Attractively boxed sets of Pinochle decks or regular double deck sets were available. The price of a twin deck box of regular cards in 1943 was $1.50.

The holiday fruit cake tin is recent, but some collectors who like to have an example of everything in Autumn Leaf are adding these to their collections. The wooden bowl shows a lot of age and the enameled design appears to be original. No information is available on its history.

Item	Introduced	Discontinued	Price
Coaster, 3 ⅛″			3.00-4.00
Hotpad, 10¾″ oval			8.00-10.00
Hotpad, 7¼″ felt back	1946		10.00-12.00
Hotpad, 7¼″ tin back	1937		6.00-8.00
Mixer cover, standard	1950	1961	20.00-25.00
Mixer cover, Mary Dunbar	1950	1961	20.00-25.00
Plastic bowl covers, 8 pc. set	1950	1961	80.00-85.00
Playing cards, regular deck	1943	1946	125.00-150.00
Playing cards, Pinochle deck	1943	1946	135.00-155.00
Toaster cover	1950	1961	20.00-25.00
Tin, holiday fruit cake			7.00-9.00
Wooden bowl			60.00-75.00
Other plastic & paper accessories not pictured:			
Melmac	1959	1962	
Cup/saucer			6.00-8.00
Plate, 7″ salad			4.00-6.00
Plate, 10″ dinner			7.00-8.00
Platter, 14″			8.00-10.00
Place mat, plastic	1940		18.00-22.00

Colorful Jewel cookbooks with Autumn Leaf china used in the illustrations.

Autumn Leaf Cloth & Paper Articles

An Autumn Leaf blanket was released by Jewel in 1979. It was made by Martex and came in three sizes and two colors. The twin size retailed for $22.99; the full size was $29.99 and the Queen/King size sold for $46.99. Another version, in addition to the standard color, is shown in the picture. This one has green leaves and lilac Autumn Leaf-style flowers.

Shelf paper was a premium which was offered in 1945. This issue of shelf paper had the pattern only on the edge and was available in sheets nine feet long and 9¼" wide. In 1956 shelf paper was again offered. This newer shelf liner was 13" wide. It was made of plastic, came in rolls 12' long, and had an all-over design.

Magnetic note holders are a Jewel premium and have been offered for many years. The set consists of five different holders. One pictures a brown panel truck, another shows an Autumn Leaf cup and saucer, a third features a coffee grinder. The remaining two depict a horse drawn vending cart and an early Jewel delivery truck.

Mary Dunbar cookbooks are a favorite collectible of many Autumn Leaf collectors. They were produced for many years. Besides the excellent recipes, they picture many pieces of Autumn Leaf.

An 18" by 30" rubber backed fatigue mat was listed in a 1958 catalog. This was intended to be used by the busy housewife to stand on while ironing or doing dishes. To date, only one of these has been reported. Therefore, the price has been listed as undetermined in the guide below.

A Jewel tablecloth with a modernistic design using Autumn Leaf colors is shown in the photo at the bottom of the next page. Due to the similarities, some Autumn Leaf collectors are beginning to search for this style tablecloth.

Item	Introduced	Discontinued	Price
Blanket, standard color, full-size	1979		50.00-65.00
Blanket, lilac color, full-size	1979		60.00-70.00
Cookbook, Mary Dunbar			8.00-10.00
Magnetic holders, set			3.00-5.00
Pickle fork			8.00-10.00
Shelf paper, pattern on edge, sheet	1945		12.00-15.00
Shelf paper, all-over pattern, roll	1956	1957	30.00-40.00
Tablecloth			UND

Items not pictured:
Fatigue mat   UND

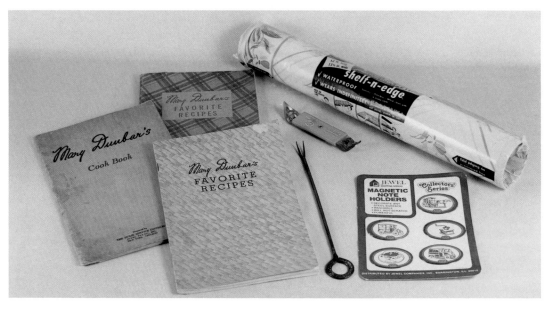

Autumn Leaf Linen & Silverware

The items shown here were not made by Hall. However they are the Autumn Leaf design and were made for the Jewel Company to complement their existing china pattern. Many collectors of china are finding these accessories are attractive additions to their collections.

Most Autumn Leaf linens, like many other collectible linens, have been subjected to many years of daily use and abuse. As a result, the availability of quality Autumn Leaf linens is limited, and prices are slowly creeping upward as more collectors are striving to add these treasures to their collections. Pieces which are stained, torn or badly faded will only bring a fraction of the prices listed below.

The muslin tablecloth and napkins were introduced as a set in 1937. The Autumn Leaf design ran just above a row of stripes along the edge and the design was repeated again in the center of the cloth. This set was discontinued in 1942.

In 1950, another tablecloth was offered. This tablecloth was plastic-coated and came in two sizes. Both sizes had an all-over Autumn Leaf design and were discontinued in 1953.

The last tablecloth introduced was made of cotton sailcloth and appeared in 1955. There were two sizes – 54 x 54 and 54 x 72. Each was decorated with a border design featuring a gold stripe below an Autumn Leaf motif.

The history of the tablecloth with the aqua, purple and yellow color is unknown. It is an interesting find and only a few of these have been reported.

Curt-towels served a dual purpose. They could be used as dish towels or curtain rods could be inserted in their wide hems to produce cafe curtains. In the photo the curt-towel is the article with the Autumn Leaf design, the cup and saucer and the clock.

In 1958, Jewel offered a silverplate flatware service made by the International Silver Company. The sets were offered in a 24-piece service for six and a 50-piece service for eight. Serving pieces which included a gravy ladle, meat fork, berry spoon and sugar shell were also available as open stock items. Autumn silverplate pieces were no longer offered after 1959, but 1960 catalogues indicate special orders would still be accepted.

Autumn pattern stainless steel tableware made by the International Silver Company craftsmen became available in 1960. Sets were available in both 24-piece and 50-piece services. A 24-piece service sold for $19.95 in 1960. Open stock items included a sugar shell and an oval soup spoon.

Item	Introduced	Discontinued	Price
Curt-towels, 4 pc. set	1957	1959	100.00-110.00
Napkin, 16" square	1937	1942	35.00-40.00
Silverware, 24 pc. silverplate set	1958	1959	350.00-400.00
Silverware, 24 pc. stainless set	1960	1968	175.00-200.00
Tablecloth, 56" x 81" muslin	1937	1942	150.00-175.00
Tablecloth, 54" x 54" plastic	1950	1953	70.00-80.00
Tablecloth, 54" x 72" plastic	1950	1953	80.00-90.00
Tablecloth, 54" x 54" sailcloth	1955	1958	60.00-70.00
Tablecloth, 54" x 72" sailcloth	1955	1958	75.00-85.00
Tea towel, 16" x 33"	1956	1957	20.00-25.00

Autumn Leaf Tin Accessories

During the last several years many new Autumn Leaf collectors have joined the ranks. These new collectors have joined with the more advanced collectors in focusing more attention on non-Hall and non-china Autumn Leaf pieces. As a result the demand for tin accessories has increased dramatically. Collectors still prefer to buy pieces in mint condition so care should be exercised when attempting to clean metal items with a lacquered finish. The finish practically dissolves when subjected to washing with water. Dealers should also remember that any pricing labels which are placed on the lacquered surface will cause damage to the finish.

The rectangular-shaped canisters on the top shelf are a four-piece set. They have plastic handles on their lids which are easily damaged. The so-called "chip resistant baked on enamel finish" is a little tougher than the coating on some of the earlier tinware, but it can also be damaged if handled carelessly.

The cleanser can is quite a prize. Any of these which are offered for sale seem to find a new home immediately.

The tin canister set in the center consists of three different size canisters. The large canister appeared in 1935, and the other two sizes followed the next year. The introduction of the smallest canister preceded the arrival of the medium-size canister by a few months. The original canister was designed to hold three pounds of coffee and sold for $.50 in 1936. The price of the three piece set was $1.00 in 1939. None of the canisters has a label to designate its contents. There are two slight variations of these sets. One style is marked "TINDECO" on the bottom and has gold lacquered insides and gold bottoms. The other style is unmarked and has a gold bottom and silver insides. The smallest canister is the most plentiful.

The round four-piece canister set introduced in 1960 had a "chip-resistant baked enamel finish" and Coppertone finish lids with black plastic knobs. The sugar and flour each hold five pounds and the coffee and tea hold 1½ pounds. The set retailed for $3.98 when it was introduced.

The picnic thermos is a hard-to-find item in good condition. Many have been destroyed by rust through the negligence of an uncaring owner. This, coupled with the war shortened production of only one year due to the scarcity of tin during World War II have combined to cause many collectors to search a long time to obtain one. The thermos has an outer jacket made of tin with a lacquered finish bearing the Autumn Leaf motif. The heavy weight of the thermos is due to the thick stoneware lining which is used for insulation.

A metal kitchen chair with a folding step was listed in a 1941 catalog. The retail price was $2.75. The chair had a baked enamel finish with the Autumn Leaf decal on the front of the backrest. War-time restrictions on the use of metals probably resulted in the production of very few of these chairs.

	Item	Introduced	Discontinued	Price
Row 1:	Canister, 8¼" sugar	1959		20.00-25.00
	Canister, 8¼" flour	1959		20.00-25.00
	Canister, 4" tea	1959		18.00-20.00
	Canister, 4" coffee	1959		18.00-20.00
	Cleanser can			150.00-175.00
Row 2:	Canister, round, 8¼"	1935	1942	25.00-30.00
	Canister, round, 7"	1935	1942	20.00-22.00
	Canister, round, 6"	1935	1942	12.00-14.00
	Sifter			100.00-120.00
Row 3:	Canister, round, tall (copper-color lid)	1960	1962	20.00-25.00
	Canister, round, short (copper-color lid)	1960	1962	15.00-18.00
	Thermos	1941	1941	150.00-175.00
	Metal accessories not pictured:			
	Chair, kitchen	1939	1942	400.00-500.00
	Tray, rectangular (red border)			45.00-50.00
	Waste basket			70.00-75.00

Autumn Leaf Tin Accessories

The lacquer finish on metal accessories was easily damaged through use and by washing. Any damage drastically reduces the desirability and value of a piece. Most collectors are seeking these metal items in "almost mint" condition.

Glass serving trays are difficult to find in good condition. They were only made for a short time, therefore they only turn up infrequently. However, to complicate matters, the design, which is painted on the reverse side of the glass, is easily damaged by water. If care is not taken in cleaning these trays, and water gets between the glass and the backing, the paint will become wrinkled, and the value of the tray will decrease substantually.

The bread box is a very desirable item for an Autumn Leaf collector to own. It was introduced in 1936 and was a casualty of the tin shortages of World War II. Bread boxes were designed to hold three regular-size loaves or two larger sandwich loaves. Since they opened conveniently from the front, they could be easily fit between two cabinet shelves. In 1938, the price of the breadbox was $1.45.

Acording to Jewel ads, the metal coffee dispenser "released the exact measure for one cup of coffee with each pull of the lever." The price of the dispenser was $2.50 in 1942 when it was discontinued. The dispenser was designed to be wall mounted and featured a glass window so the remaining quantity of coffee could be determined easily. Its war-curtailed production has caused this item to be in short supply today.

Two different styles of cake safes are available to the collector. The older one was released in 1935 and has the Autumn Leaf pattern on top as well as on the side of the lid. It sold for $1.25 in 1936. The newer one was issued in 1950 and lacks the pattern on the top of the lid. Both cake safes were equipped with a locking handle and were designed to carry a standard 9" cake placed on the matching Jewel Autumn Leaf cakeplate. Notice also, the lighter color of the older cakesafe, which is characteristic of the pre-war tinware.

	Item	Introduced	Discontinued	Price
Row 1:	Glass tray	1975	1976	65.00-75.00
Row 2:	Bread box	1937	1941	150.00-175.00
	Coffee dispenser	1941	1941	75.00-85.00
Row 3:	Cake safe	1950	1953	15.00-18.00
	Cake safe	1935	1941	27.00-32.00
	Below: Tray, 18¾" oval	1934	1938	35.00-42.00

Complete coffee service first offered in 1934.

Glasbake & Porcelain-Clad Steel Cookware & Bakeware

Autumn design porcelain-clad steel cookware was a Jewel exclusive which was introduced in 1979. The cookware set consists of seven pieces. It includes a 1½-quart covered saucepan, a 2-quart covered saucepan, a 5-quart covered Dutch oven and a 9½" open skillet. The Dutch oven cover also fits the skillet. Retail price for this set was $59.95. Also, offered at the same time was a matching teakettle which sold for $16.95. By the next year the price of the teakettle had increased to $18.99.

In 1980, Jewel added three new sets to complement its original offering. All were made of the familiar enameled porcelain metal which was supposed to be chip resistant and easy to clean.

A three-piece mixing bowl set consists of bowls in the 1⅓-quart, 2-quart and 2⅔-quart sizes. This set and a 2-quart fondue set were priced at $29.99 each. The fondue set consists of a 2-quart pot with a brown metal cover, a metal rack with a fork stand, six colored coded forks, a chrome-plated burner and a brown metal tray.

The rectangular pieces of the bakeware/casserole set came in 1-quart, 2-quart and 3-quart sizes. They were conveniently designed so the same dish could be utilized for cooking, serving and the storing of leftovers. The casseroles had tab handles for easy handling and featured plastic storage lids which snapped on tightly to ensure the safekeeping of leftovers.

The Glasbake articles shown on the two shelves below are part of a short-lived bakeware set introduced in 1961. The set consists of a divided oval bowl, two sizes of covered casseroles and a four-piece bowl set. These items were not very popular and were only offered for one season.

	Cookware/Bakeware	Price
Row 1:	Dutch oven, 5-quart	25.00-30.00
	Fondue set	45.00-55.00
Row 2:	Saucepan, 2-quart	18.00-22.00
	Saucepan, 1½-quart	15.00-18.00
Row 3:	Mixing bowl, 2⅔-quart	12.00-15.00
	Mixing bowl, 2-quart	10.00-12.00
	Mixing bowl, 1⅓-quart	9.00-10.00
Row 4:	Tea kettle	50.00-60.00
	Bakeware/casserole set, 3-piece	40.00-45.00
Below:	Casserole, Glasbake	15.00-18.00
	Divided bowl, Glasbake	12.00-15.00
	Bowl set, 4-piece, Glasbake	30.00-35.00
	Not pictured	
	Skillet, 9"	15.00-18.00

Autumn Leaf Glass & Metal Accessories

Glassware with the Autumn Leaf motif continues to be popular among collectors. The most desirable items are those pictured on the top row, however the Douglas pieces are becoming increasingly collectible although many collectors are finding them prohibitively expensive.

The exciting news in this area is that a new style frosted tumbler has been found. It is a 6½" tall pilsner-shape tumbler with frosted sides and a clear bottom. The bottom has the Libbey "L" mark and the sides have the all-over Autumn design. The bad news for collectors is that this is a sample item which was never offered by sale by Jewel. Therefore, only handful of collectors can ever hope to own one of these pieces.

The frosted tumblers on the first row were made for Jewel by Libbey. The tumbler with the bands at the bottom is the hardest to find. Of the two frosted tumblers with the Autumn Leaf motif, the large one is the easiest to find. A set of six of the large tumblers sold for $1.98 in 1949.

The clear tumblers on the top shelf with the Autumn-like design were made by Brockway. The tumblers were offered in three sizes and disappeared quickly from Jewel's catalogue after a short trial in the mid-1970's. As a result of the short run, these tumblers are not easy to find and they are expensive for a "newer" item.

The clear tumblers on the second shelf were made for Jewel by Libbey in the early 1960's. These tumblers were advertised as having "an all-over Autumn pattern in 22K gold and etched frost motif with Safedege Gold rims which defy chipping." The four pieces offered consisted of two sizes of heavy bottom tumblers, a footed goblet and a footed sherbet. A set of eight tumblers sold for $3.98 and sets of sherbets or goblets were $5.98.

The first Autumn pattern Douglas piece – a combination coffee percolator, carafe and candle warmer – appeared in Jewel's 1960 catalogue. It had a 22K gold fused design, a bakelite handle and an anodized aluminum lid and collar. Like many other Jewel items this was a multi-purpose piece. It was presented as an eight-cup percolator, or a 12-cup instant coffee maker, tea maker or beverage server. Other Douglas pieces which were introduced the following year include a sauce dish with a candle warmer base and hurricane lamps with goldtone metal bases. Several collectors have reported finding an unlisted ice lip style pitcher which is similar in shape and size to the eight-cup coffee maker. To postively identify the Douglas Autumn pattern items look for the name "Douglas" stamped in gold near the bottom of the piece.

Jewel customers remember the metal canisters with the plastic lids coming filled with Old Fashioned hard Christmas candy. The goldtone candlesticks pictured on the third shelf also are used as the base for the footed cakeplate and footed candy shown on page 35.

	Item	Introduced	Discontinued	Price
Row 1:	Tumbler, banded			20.00-22.00
	Tumbler, 5½" frosted	1940	1949	10.00-12.00
	Tumbler, 3¾" frosted	1950	1953	16.00-18.00
	Tumbler, 16 oz. Brockway	1975	1976	18.00-20.00
	Tumbler, 13 oz. Brockway	1975	1976	15.00-17.00
	Tumbler, 9 oz. Brockway	1975	1976	13.00-15.00
Row 2:	Tumbler, 15 oz. Libbey	1960	1961	25.00-30.00
	Tumbler, 10 oz. Libbey	1958	1961	20.00-25.00
	Goblet, 10 oz. Libbey	1960	1961	30.00-35.00
	Sherbet, 6½ oz. Libbey	1960	1961	30.00-35.00
	Sauce dish, Douglas	1961	1962	65.00-85.00
	Warmer base	1960	1962	15.00-20.00
Row 3:	Percolator, Douglas	1960	1962	100.00-125.00
	Canister, brown/gold			8.00-10.00
	Canister, white plastic lid			7.00-9.00
	Candlestick, pair			30.00-40.00
Not pictured				
	Hurricane lamp, Douglas, pair	1961	1962	175.00-200.00
	Pitcher, Douglas ice lip			UND

Rare frosted Autumn leaf pilsner-style tumbler.

Blue Bouquet

Hall China produced this decal line for the Standard Coffee Company of New Orleans, therefore, Blue Bouquet is a pattern which is found more frequently in the southeastern states. Production was begun in the early 1950's and continued into the mid-1960's. All pieces of the D-style dinnerware may be found. Many china kitchenware pieces exist, and there are a limited number of metal accessories available.

Among the more frequently found pieces are the large salad bowl, the drip jar, the handled shakers, sugars and creamers and the #3 "Medallion" jug. Hard-to-find pieces include the New England bean pot, the pretzel jar, the electric percolator, both leftovers, the soup tureen and the spoon. Notice the special heating element on the electric percolator which fits between the base and the china dripper.

Metal kitchen items with the Blue Bouquet decal include canisters, coasters, shakers and a coffee dispenser.

The photo below pictures tumbler prototypes with the Blue Bouquet decal. The tumblers were found in the Toledo area which is the home of Libbey. Yellow markings on the tumblers suggest their former home may have been in the company's sample department. The two tumblers to the left are frosted. However, the one on the left has a narrow clear band around the top. The tumbler in the center is clear and the one on the right is frosted on the bottom half and clear on the top. Since other tumblers are not being found it is probably safe to assume these samples did not meet with approval and were never put into production.

The photo at the bottom of page 52 pictures a "Kadota" style all-china coffee pot and the six cup Boston teapot. Both pieces are hard-to-find and are new to the kitchenware listing.

D-Style Dinnerware	Price
Bowl, 5½" fruit	3.50-4.00
Bowl, 6" cereal	5.00-6.00
Bowl, 8½" flat soup	10.00-12.00
Bowl, 9¼" round vegetable	20.00-22.00
Cup	4.00-5.00
Gravy boat	20.00-22.00
Plate, 6"	2.00-2.50
Plate, 8¼"	6.00-7.00
Plate, 7¼"	4.00-5.00
Plate, 9"	7.00-9.00
Platter, 11¼" oval	14.00-16.00
Platter, 13¼" oval	16.00-18.00
Saucer	1.00-1.50

Prototype Blue bouquet tumblers made by Libbey.
Left to right: 1. Lower ¾ frosted, top ¼ clear; 2. entire tumbler frosted; 3. entire tumbler clear, 4. bottom ½ frosted with clear bands, top ½ clear.

Row 1: Sugar and creamer, Boston; salad bowl, 9″; sugar and creamer; modern. **Row 2:** Drip jar, "Thick Rim," salt and pepper, handled; cup and saucer. **Row 3:** Bowl, flat soup; bowl, 6″ cereal; bowl, 5½″ fruit. **Row 4:** Plate, 9″ dinner; plate, 8¼″; plate 6″. **Row 5:** Platter, 13″ oval, bowl, 7¾″ flared; custard, "Thick Rim."

Kitchenware	Price
Baker, French fluted	15.00-18.00
Ball jug #3	20.00-25.00
Bean pot, New England #4	60.00-75.00
Bowl, 7¾″ flared	18.00-20.00
Bowl, 9″ salad	14.00-16.00
Bowl, 6″ "Radiance"	8.00-10.00
Bowl, 7½″ "Radiance"	12.00-14.00
Bowl, 9″ "Radiance"	16.00-18.00
Bowl, 6″ "Thick Rim"	8.00-10.00
Bowl, 7½″ "Thick Rim"	14.00-16.00
Bowl, 8½″ "Thick Rim"	16.00-18.00
Cakeplate	14.00-16.00
Casserole, "Radiance"	25.00-30.00
Casserole, "Thick Rim"	25.00-28.00
Coffee pot, "Five Band"	45.00-50.00
Coffee pot, "Terrace"	40.00-45.00
Creamer, Boston	6.00-8.00
Creamer, modern	6.00-8.00
Custard	4.00-5.00
Drip coffee pot, "Kadota" all-china	125.00-150.00
Drip jar, "Thick Rim"	16.00-18.00
Electric percolator	150.00-175.00
Jug, "Medallion" #3	12.00-14.00
Leftover, rectangular	22.00-25.00
Leftover, square	32.00-35.00
Pie baker	16.00-18.00
Pretzel jar	60.00-70.00
Shakers, teardrop, ea.	7.00-8.00
Shakers, handled, ea.	8.00-9.00
Spoon	32.00-37.00
Soup tureen	75.00-85.00
Sugar and lid, Boston	10.00-12.00
Sugar and lid, modern	10.00-12.00
Teapot, Aladdin, round lid with infusor	45.00-50.00
Teapot, Boston	50.00-60.00

Left: Drip coffee pot, "Kadota" shape all china. **Right:** Boston teapot.

Row 1: Pretzel jar; bean pot, New England #4; coffee pot, "Terrace." **Row 2:** Ball jug #3; teapot with infusor, Aladdin; coffee pot, "Five Band." **Row 3:** Soup tureen; jug, "Medallion" #3; casserole, "Thick Rim." **Row 4:** Electric percolator; coffee dispenser; metal canisters.

Crocus

Crocus is a Hall dinnerware pattern which was introduced in the mid-1930's. Assembling the multitude of pieces available in this pattern presents a challenge to even the most dedicated collectors. Obtaining basic dinnerware pieces, which appear to be in short supply, is frustrating to some of the collectors who do not have access to major shows or flea markets.

The list of new shapes appearing with the Crocus decal continues to expand. Even some veteran Hall collectors have been astounded by some of the recent discoveries in this pattern. Some of the more exciting discoveries include the Donut shape teapot, the teardrop-style shakers, and a new style coffee pot with a metal dripper which collectors are calling "Meltdown." In addition, just to keep collectors interested and to add a little confusion, there are two styles of all-china drip coffee pots, two different shape beverage mugs and at least five different shapes of coffee pots with the Drip-O-lator backstamp. One of these is a shaped called "Kadota" which we have only seen with a china dripper. The other four have a metal dripper which usually has the Crocus decal embossed on it. The "Five Band" coffee pot also will be found with a glass dripper which contains an electric heating element.

Two other pieces with the Crocus decal which are new in this edition include the Aladdin and Streamline teapots. Both of these are very hard-to-find.

Several "Zephyr" style one-pound butter dishes and leftovers have been reported since the last book, but these pieces are still lacking from many collections. The matching water bottle is not being found as frequently. Notice the two different shapes of beverage mugs – 8 ounce flagon and tankard style. The lid to the tureen may be found smooth or with an embossed clover shape. A variation of the set of straight-sided bowls may sometimes be found with blue exteriors. These bowls have the Crocus decal on their white interior surface.

A metal piece, the soap dispenser, was overlooked previously and is now in the listing. This piece is not rare, but is seldom found in good condition.

D-style Dinnerware	Price	D-style Dinnerware	Price
Bowl, 5½″ fruit	3.00-4.00	Plate, 7¼″	4.00-6.00
Bowl, 6″ cereal	6.00-8.00	Plate, 8¼″	6.00-8.00
Bowl, 8½″ flat soup	9.00-11.00	Plate, 9″	7.00-9.00
Bowl, 9¼″ round vegetable	18.00-20.00	Plate, 10″	12.00-15.00
Bowl, oval	16.00-18.00	Platter, 11¼″ oval	14.00-16.00
Cup	5.00-7.00	Platter, 13¼″ oval	16.00-18.00
Gravy boat	18.00-20.00	Saucer	1.00-2.00
Plate, 6″	2.00-3.00	Tidbit, 3-tier	35.00-40.00

Mug, beverage (flagon style); teapot, Streamline; teapot, Aladdin; shakers, teardrop style.

Row 1: Drip coffee pot, "Kadota"; ball jug #3. **Row 2:** Bowl, 9″ round; cup and saucer. **Row 3:** Custard, "Radiance;" leftover, square; bowl, 5½″ fruit. **Row 4:** Plate, 6″; Plate, 9″; bowl, flat soup. **Row 5:** Tray, oval, metal.

Row 1: Drip coffee, "Jordan;" coffee pot, "Meltdown." **Row 2:** Coffee pot, "Waverly;" teapot, Donut.

Kitchenware	Price
Baker, French fluted	18.00-20.00
Ball jug #3	30.00-35.00
Bean pot, New England #4	65.00-70.00
Bowl, 9″ salad	14.00-16.00
Bowl, 6″ "Radiance"	7.00-9.00
Bowl, 7½″ "Radiance"	10.00-12.00
Bowl, 9″ "Radiance"	14.00-16.00
Butter, one pound "Zephyr"-style	350.00-400.00
Cakeplate	16.00-18.00
Casserole, "Radiance"	22.00-25.00
Coffee pot*, "Five Band"	32.00-37.00
Coffee pot, "Medallion"	35.00-40.00
Coffee pot, "Meltdown"	40.00-50.00
Coffee pot, "Terrace" (two sizes)	22.00-27.00
Coffee pot, "Waverly" (Drip-O-lator)	27.00-30.00
Creamer, Art Deco	8.00-10.00
Creamer, "Medallion"	10.00-12.00
Creamer, "Meltdown"	12.00-15.00
Creamer, modern	6.00-8.00
Creamer, New York	10.00-12.00
Cup, St. Denis	16.00-18.00
Custard	7.00-8.00
Drip coffee pot, "Jordan"	175.00-200.00
Drip coffee pot, "Kadota"	95.00-125.00
Drip jar, #1188 open	22.00-25.00
Drip jar and lid, "Radiance"	16.00-18.00
Jug and cover, "Radiance" #3, #4	45.00-50.00
Jug and cover, "Radiance" #5, #6	50.00-65.00
Jug, "Simplicity"	75.00-85.00

Kitchenware	Price
Leftover, rectangular	19.00-22.00
Leftover, square	22.00-25.00
Leftover, "Zephyr"-style	150.00-175.00
Mug, flagon style	32.00-35.00
Mug, tankard style	25.00-28.00
Pie baker	16.00-18.00
Pretzel jar	60.00-70.00
Saucer, St Denis	4.00-5.00
Shakers, handled ea.	7.00-8.00
Shakers, teardrop, ea.	12.00-14.00
Soup tureen, plain or clover lid	85.00-95.00
Stack set, "Radiance"	45.00-55.00
Sugar and lid, Art Deco	10.00-12.00
Sugar and lid, "Medallion"	12.00-14.00
Sugar and lid, "Meltdown"	18.00-20.00
Sugar and lid, modern	10.00-12.00
Sugar and lid, New York	12.00-14.00
Teapot, Aladdin	65.00-75.00
Teapot, Boston	60.00-65.00
Teapot, Donut	UND
Teapot, "Medallion"	25.00-30.00
Teapot, New York	30.00-35.00
Teapot, Streamline	150.00-200.00
Teapot, two cup "Terrace"	55.00-60.00
Water bottle, "Zephyr"-style	125.00-150.00

Metal Accessories

Soap dispenser	22.00-25.00
Tray, oval	18.00-22.00

*With glass dripper   62.00-67.00

Row 1: Gravy boat; bean pot, New England #4; sugar, Art Deco style; creamer, Art Deco style. **Row 2:** Butter, ''Zephyr'';
leftover, ''Zephyr''; leftover, rectangular. **Row 3:** Drip jar, ''Radiance''; salt and pepper, handled; mug, beverage. **Row 4:** Teapot, New York; soup tureen, tidbit, 3-tier.

Mums

Mums is a pink floral decal which appers to be most prevalent in the Wisconsin and Minnesota areas. The earliest references to this decal date to the late 1930's. Many people seem to be confusing this decal with another similar decal – Pastel Morning Glory. There are substantial differences between the two decals if care is taken to look at them closely. Even if the obvious difference between the two types of flowers is ignored, Mums does not have the sprigs of blue flowers which are present on the Pastel Morning Glory pieces.

All pieces of the D-shaped dinnerware have been found, and the kitchenware listing continues to expand. However, this pattern is almost impossible to collect unless you live in one of the two states mentioned above.

New discoveries include a six-cup New York teapot, and its matching covered sugar and creamer, a large round ruffled "Medallion" bowl, and the "Simplicity" jug. The large size "Medallion" teapot is shown in the photograph. We have not heard any reports of the smaller one appearing with this decal.

Left to right: Pretzel jar; jug, "Simplicity;" open drip jar, #1188.

D-style Dinnerware	Price
Bowl, 5½″ fruit	3.00-4.00
Bowl, 6″ cereal	5.00-6.00
Bowl, 8½″ flat soup	6.00-8.00
Bowl, 9¼″ round	14.00-16.00
Bowl, 10¼″ oval	14.00-16.00
Cup	5.00-6.00
Plate, 6″	2.50-3.50
Plate, 8¼″	4.50-5.00
Plate, 9″	7.00-8.00
Platter, 11¼″ oval	12.00-14.00
Platter, 13¼″ oval	14.00-16.00
Saucer	1.00-2.00

Kitchenware	Price
Bowl, 9″ salad	10.00-12.00
Bowl, 6″ "Radiance"	6.00-8.00
Bowl, 7½″ "Radiance"	8.00-10.00
Bowl, 9″ "Radiance"	10.00-12.00
Bowl, 9½″ ruffled, tab-handled "Medallion"	35.00-40.00
Casserole, "Medallion"	30.00-35.00
Casserole, "Radiance"	30.00-35.00
Coffee pot, "Medallion"	35.00-40.00
Coffee pot, "Terrace"	35.00-40.00
Creamer, Art Deco	10.00-12.00
Creamer, "Medallion"	8.00-10.00

Kitchenware	Price	Kitchenware	Price
Creamer, New York	8.00-10.00	Shakers, handled, ea.	8.00-9.00
Custard	4.00-5.00	Stack set, "Radiance"	45.00-55.00
Drip jar, #1188 open	22.00-27.00	Sugar and lid, Art Deco	12.00-14.00
Drip jar and cover, "Medallion"	16.00-18.00	Sugar and lid, "Medallion"	10.00-12.00
Jug, #3 "Medallion"	22.00-25.00	Sugar and lid, New York	10.00-12.00
Jug, "Simplicity"	60.00-65.00	Teapot, "Medallion"	30.00-35.00
Mug, beverage	28.00-32.00	Teapot, New York	40.00-45.00
Pie baker	18.00-20.00	Teapot, "Rutherford"	50.00-60.00
Pretzel jar	55.00-60.00		

Row 1: Teapot, "Medallion;" sugar and creamer, "Medallion;" teapot, "Rutherford."
Row 2: Shakers, handled; drip jar, "Medallion;" beverage mug, tankard style. **Row 3:** Sugar and creamer, New York; cup and saucer; gravy boat. **Row 4:** Casserole, "Medallion;" bowl, 9¼″ round; bowl, 5½″ fruit. **Row 5:** Pie baker; bowl, 8½″ flat soup.

No. 488

Numerous new kitchenware shapes with this decal and the discovery of the existence of Hall dinnerware have made this pattern more attractive to collect. All of the dinnerware seems to be concentrated in the Wisconsin and Minnesota areas, while kitchenware seems to be found both there and in eastern Pennsylvania. Although it is not rare, a complete set of dinnerware will be difficult to assemble.

Interesting new kitchenware finds include the "Zephyr" style butter, teardrop shakers and the "Radiance" condiment jar. Notice in the picture the teardrop shakers may be difficult to identify since they only have a small part of the No. 488 decal. The lids to all the sizes of "Radiance" jugs exist, but it will take diligent searching to find both the largest and the smallest.

As usual, some discoveries provide a ray of hope that other unconfirmed pieces will soon come to light. The existence of the canisters leads us to believe the canister-style shakers will eventually be found. Note the appearance of the Tom and Jerry mug. This mug led to the search for the confirmation of the existence of the punch bowl. Sure enough, bowls have been found, but they are a very rare find.

Row 1: Stack set, "Radiance;" jug, #5 "Radiance;" casserole, "Radiance." **Row 2:** Jug and cover, #3 "Radiance;" shirred egg dish; shakers, "Novelty Radiance;" custard, "Radiance."

D-style Dinnerware	Price
Bowl, 5½″ fruit	3.50-4.00
Bowl, 8½″ flat soup	10.00-12.00
Cup	7.00-8.00
Plate, 7″	4.00-5.00
Plate, 8¼″	4.00-5.00
Plate, 9″	6.00-8.00
Platter, 11¼″ oval	12.00-14.00
Platter, 13¼″ oval	16.00-18.00
Saucer	1.50-2.00

Kitchenware	Price
Ball jug #3	22.00-25.00
Bean pot, New England (#3, #4, #5)	50.00-60.00
Bowl, 6″ "Radiance"	8.00-10.00
Bowl, 7½″ "Radiance"	10.00-12.00
Bowl, 9″ "Radiance"	12.00-14.00
Butter, 1# "Zephyr"	300.00-350.00
Canister, "Radiance"	90.00-110.00
Casserole, "Five Band"	30.00-32.00
Casserole, "Medallion"	30.00-35.00
Casserole, "Radiance"	25.00-30.00
Casserole, "Sundial"	32.00-35.00
Casserole, "Thick Rim"	30.00-35.00
Coffee pot, "Meltdown"	45.00-55.00
Condiment jar, "Radiance"	150.00-200.00
Cookie jar, "Five Band"	55.00-65.00
Creamer, Art Deco	8.00-10.00
Creamer, modern	7.00-9.00
Custard	4.00-5.00
Drip coffee pot, "Radiance"	125.00-150.00
Drip jar, #1188 open	16.00-18.00
Drip jar and cover, "Medallion"	18.00-20.00
Drip jar and cover, "Radiance"	18.00-20.00
Jug, "Medallion" ice lip	35.00-40.00
Jug and cover, "Radiance" (#2, #3)	45.00-55.00
Jug and cover, "Radiance" (#4, #5, #6)	55.00-65.00
Leftover, square	45.00-50.00
Mug, Tom & Jerry	10.00-12.00
Pretzel jar	80.00-90.00
Punch bowl, Tom & Jerry	UND
Shakers, handled, ea.	9.00-10.00
Shakers, "Medallion," ea.	14.00-16.00
Shakers, "Novelty Radiance," ea.	14.00-16.00
Shakers, teardrop, ea.	10.00-12.00
Shirred egg dish	25.00-28.00
Soup tureen	95.00-110.00
Stack set, "Radiance"	65.00-75.00
Sugar and lid, Art Deco	12.00-14.00
Sugar and lid, modern	10.00-12.00
Teapot, New York	80.00-90.00
Teapot, "Radiance"	90.00-110.00

Row 1: Pretzel jar; Ball jug #3; teapot, "Radiance." **Row 2:** Soup tureen; casserole, "Sundial"; bean pot, New England #3. **Row 3:** Shakers, teardrop style; leftover, square; drip jar, #1188 open. **Row 4:** Butter, one pound "Zephyr-style"; mug, Tom & Jerry; sugar and creamer, Art Deco.

Orange Poppy

Orange Poppy is a decal dinnerware line which was introduced in 1933. Production continued through the 1950's, and the pattern was used as a premium for the Great American Tea Company. The Great American Tea Company logo may be seen in the dinnerware backstamps pictured on page 64.

Until recently, C-style dinnerware appeared to be abundant, but newer collectors are reporting shortages of plates, cups and saucers. Items which are hardest to find include the spoon, canister-style shakers and the Bellvue-shape teapot and coffee pot. Other desirable pieces which many collectors are still seeking are the canister set, the Melody and Donut teapots.

The few metal accessories available in this pattern are not abundant, but most collectors who are patient and persistent will be able to find these items. Notice the canister set is square, but the shakers are round. The cake safe shown has a metal cover and a wooden base.

C-style Dinnerware	Price
Bowl, 5½″ fruit	3.50-4.00
Bowl, 6″ cereal	5.00-7.00
Bowl, 8½″ flat soup	8.00-10.00
Bowl, 9¼″ round vegetable	15.00-20.00
Cup	5.00-7.00
Plate, 6″	3.00-4.00
Plate, 7¾″	5.00-6.00
Plate, 9″	7.00-8.00
Platter, 11¼″ oval	14.00-16.00
Platter, 13¼″ oval	16.00-18.00
Saucer	1.50-2.00

Teapot, 2-cup Bellvue.

Cake safe.

Kitchenware	Price	Kitchenware	Price
Baker, French fluted	14.00-16.00	Pretzel jar	60.00-65.00
Ball jug #3	20.00-25.00	Shakers, teardrop, ea.	8.00-10.00
Bean pot, New England #4	45.00-50.00	Shakers, handled, ea.	8.00-9.00
Bowl, 6″ "Radiance"	8.00-10.00	Shakers, canister-style "Radiance," ea.	40.00-50.00
Bowl, 7½″ "Radiance"	12.00-14.00	Shakers, "Novelty Radiance," ea.	18.00-20.00
Bowl, 9″ "Radiance"	14.00-16.00	Spoon	40.00-45.00
Bowl, 10″ "Radiance"	22.00-25.00	Sugar and lid, "Great American"	9.00-11.00
Bowl, salad	12.00-14.00	Teapot, 2-cup Bellvue	95.00-110.00
Cakeplate	10.00-12.00	Teapot, Boston	45.00-55.00
Canister, "Radiance"	70.00-75.00	Teapot, Donut	110.00-125.00
Casserole, 8″ oval	22.00-25.00	Teapot, Melody	90.00-100.00
Casserole, 11¾″ oval	55.00-65.00	Teapot, Streamline	55.00-65.00
Casserole, 13″ oval	75.00-85.00	Teapot, Windshield	75.00-85.00
Casserole, #76 round	22.00-25.00		
Coffee pot, 2-cup Bellvue	95.00-110.00		
Coffee pot, "Great American"	35.00-40.00	**Metal Accessories**	**Price**
Coffee pot, S-lid	35.00-40.00	Bread box	30.00-35.00
Condiment jar, "Radiance"	150.00-200.00	Cake safe	20.00-25.00
Creamer, "Great American"	8.00-10.00	Canister set, 4 pc.	35.00-40.00
Custard	3.00-4.00	Coffee dispenser	14.00-17.00
Drip jar and cover, "Radiance"	16.00-18.00	Match safe	18.00-20.00
Jug, #4 "Radiance"	18.00-20.00	Shakers, ea.	4.00-6.00
Jug, #5 "Radiance"	14.00-16.00	Sifter	20.00-25.00
Leftover, loop handle	30.00-34.00	Soap dispenser	30.00-35.00
Mustard and liner	32.00-37.00	Tray, oval	18.00-22.00
Pie baker	18.00-20.00	Waste basket	30.00-35.00

Early Orange Poppy Dinnerware backstamp.

Orange Poppy Dinnerware backstamp used in 1956.

Row 1: Sugar and creamer, "Great American"; mustard, 3 pc. set; custard. **Row 2:** Bowl, "Radiance" #5; bowl, 9″ round; bowl, 5½″ fruit. **Row 3:** Bowl, 9″ salad; cakeplate; plate, 9″ dinner. **Row 4:** Spoon; cup and saucer; salt and pepper, metal. **Row 5:** Canister set, 4 pc. metal.

Row 1: Coffee pot, S-lid; coffee pot, "Great American"; coffee pot, 2-cup Bellvue. **Row 2:** Teapot, Melody; teapot, Donut; ball jug #3. **Row 3:** Pretzel jar; bean pot, New England #4; casserole, 8″ oval. **Row 4:** Salt, handled; drip jar, "Radiance"; pepper, handled; leftover, loop handled; canister, "Radiance."

Pastel Morning Glory

The Pastel Morning Glory pattern provides an attractive dinnerware service. The decal features a prominent pink morning glory accented with tiny blue floral sprigs and green leaves. This decal appears to be of late 1930's origin and the pattern was distributed primarily in upper Michigan, Wisconsin and Minnesota. Collectors living in these areas seem to find an ample supply of items; those in other parts of the country have trouble finding even the most common pieces.

Some interesting items have appeared since the last book. Among these is the Donut jug which is rarely found with any decal. The square and rectangular leftovers are also prize pieces. Covered jugs are still in short supply, but more are turning up. Teapots and coffee pots have also been added to the list of items appearing with this decal. This has made teapot and coffee pot collectors happy, in addition to pleasing Pastel Morning Glory collectors.

D-style Dinnerware	Price
Bowl, 5½″ fruit	3.50-4.00
Bowl, 6″ cereal	5.00-6.00
Bowl, 8½″ flat soup	8.00-10.00
Bowl, 9¼″ round	14.00-16.00
Bowl, oval	14.00-16.00
Cup	5.00-6.00
Gravy boat	18.00-20.00
Plate, 6″	2.50-3.00
Plate, 7¼″	4.00-5.00
Plate, 8¼″	5.00-6.00
Plate, 9″	7.00-8.00
Plate, 10″	9.00-11.00
Platter, 11¼″	12.00-14.00
Platter, 13¼″	16.00-18.00
Saucer	1.00-1.50

Kitchenware	Price
Ball jug #3	25.00-30.00
Bean pot, New England #4	55.00-60.00
Bowl, 9″ salad	10.00-12.00
Bowl, 6″ "Radiance"	6.00-8.00
Bowl, 7½″ "Radiance"	8.00-10.00
Bowl, 9″ "Radiance"	10.00-12.00
Cakeplate	14.00-16.00
Casserole, "Medallion"	25.00-30.00

Kitchenware	Price
Casserole, "Radiance"	25.00-28.00
Coffee pot, "Terrace"	40.00-45.00
Creamer, Art Deco	10.00-12.00
Creamer, modern	6.00-8.00
Creamer, New York	8.00-10.00
Cup, St Denis	12.00-14.00
Custard	4.00-5.00
Drip jar and lid, "Radiance"	16.00-18.00
Drip jar, #1188 open	22.00-25.00
Jug, Donut	75.00-85.00
Jug and cover, #4, #5, #6 "Radiance"	45.00-55.00
Leftover, rectangular	20.00-22.00
Leftover, square	25.00-30.00
Pie baker	16.00-18.00
Pretzel jar	60.00-70.00
Saucer, St Denis	3.50-4.50
Shakers, handled, ea.	7.00-9.00
Shakers, "Novelty Radiance," ea.	14.00-18.00
Shakers, teardrop, ea.	8.00-10.00
Stack set, "Radiance"	45.00-55.00
Sugar and lid, Art Deco	12.00-14.00
Sugar and lid, modern	10.00-12.00
Sugar and lid, New York	10.00-12.00
Teapot, Aladdin	45.00-50.00
Teapot, New York	40.00-45.00
Teapot, "Rutherford"	45.00-50.00

Row 1: Teapot, "Rutherford"; coffee pot, "Terrace"; teapot, New York. **Row 2:** Ball jug #3; jug and cover, #4 "Radiance"; sugar and creamer, modern. **Row 3:** Shakers, handled; drip jar, #1188 open; gravy boat; creamer, Art Deco. **Row 4:** Casserole, "Radiance"; bowl, 6″ "Radiance;" pie baker. **Row 5:** Cup and saucer; platter, 11¼″ oval; bowl 5½″ fruit.

Red Poppy

Hall's Red Poppy pattern consists of a red floral decal accented with black leaves using an ivory body as a background. Additionally, each piece is highlighted with a narrow silver band. Production of this pattern began in the mid-1930's and continued for about 20 years. The Grand Union Tea Company, which used this pattern as a premium, was the primary recipient of this lengthy production.

Although the D-style dinnerware pieces are general-ly available for moderate prices, both the quantity and quality of available items appears to be shrinking. The serving pieces have become especially popular and usually sell very quickly. The gravy boat lacks an underplate and is not an easily found item. Cups may be found with their decal on either the inside or on the outside. Collectors are experiencing a lot of frustration trying to locate 10″ dinner plates. The 9″ dinner plate is the most commonly found size of plate.

D-style Dinnerware	Price
Bowl, 5½″ fruit	3.50-4.00
Bowl, 6″ cereal	6.00-7.00
Bowl, 8½″ round	8.00-10.00
Bowl, 9¼″ round	16.00-18.00
Bowl, 10¼″ oval	14.00-16.00
Cup	6.00-7.00
Gravy boat	18.00-20.00
Plate, 6″	2.00-3.00

D-style Dinnerware	Price
Plate, 7¼″	3.00-4.50
Plate, 8¼″	4.00-6.00
Plate, 9″	6.00-8.00
Plate, 10″	12.00-14.00
Platter, 11¼″ oval	14.00-16.00
Platter, 13¼″ oval	16.00-18.00
Saucer	1.00-1.50

"Daniel" coffee pot with metal dripper.

Red Poppy

China kitchenware accessory pieces in Red Poppy appear to be limited to the "bare essentials." There does not appear to be the variety of shapes and sizes of such premium articles like coffee pots, teapots or cookie jars which are found in some of the other popular Hall patterns. Also, while interesting pieces are being uncovered in other patterns, only one new china piece has been reported in this pattern in the last four years. This is a taller version of the "Daniel" shape creamer which appears to be either a milk jug or syrup.

Notice the slight difference in color of the Aladdin teapot and the French baker in comparison to the other pieces in the photo. On these two articles, the Red Poppy decal has been placed on a Hi-white body. This deviation from the use of an ivory body may indicate that these two items were made for some company other than Grand Union.

Kitchenware	Price
Baker, French fluted	14.00-16.00
Ball jug #3	28.00-30.00
Bowl, 9″ salad	12.00-14.00
Bowl, 6″ "Radiance"	6.00-8.00
Bowl, 7½″ "Radiance"	8.00-10.00
Bowl, 9″ "Radiance"	10.00-12.00
Cakeplate	10.00-12.00
Casserole, "Radiance"	20.00-22.00
Coffee pot, "Daniel"	22.00-27.00
Creamer, "Daniel"	6.00-8.00
Creamer, modern	6.00-8.00
Custard	5.00-7.00
Drip jar, #1188 open	22.00-27.00

Kitchenware	Price
Drip jar and cover, "Radiance"	14.00-16.00
Jug, 4″ "Daniel" milk or syrup	22.00-25.00
Jug, #5 "Radiance"	14.00-16.00
Leftover, square	25.00-30.00
Pie baker	16.00-18.00
Shakers, teardrop, ea.	8.00-9.00
Shakers, handled, ea.	7.00-8.50
Sugar and lid, "Daniel"	10.00-12.00
Sugar and lid, modern	10.00-12.00
Teapot, Aladdin with oval infusor and lid	50.00-55.00
Teapot, New York	40.00-45.00

Row 1: "Daniel" creamer; "Daniel" milk jug or syrup. **Row 2:** Cakesafe; look-alike waffle iron.

Row 1: Coffee pot, "Daniel"; sugar and creamer, "Daniel"; jug, "Radiance" #5. **Row 2:** Teapot, New York; teapot, Aladdin; salt, handled; drip jar, "Radiance"; pepper, handled. **Row 3:** Casserole, "Radiance"; baker, French; drip jar, #1188 open; custard, "Radiance." **Row 4:** Bowl, "Radiance" #5; bowl, "Radiance" #4; bowl, "Radiance" #3.

Red Poppy

Glass accessory items in the Red Poppy pattern consist of a 10-ounce frosted tumbler with two styles of decal, a clear tumbler and a one-gallon canister. Of these glass items, the clear tumbler is the hardest to find. The gallon canister is a square clear glass jar with a screw lid and red poppies painted on the outside with enamel. This jar is also sometimes found with green enameled poppies. Two styles of frosted tumblers are shown in the picture on page 74. One style is slightly taller than the other, the flower is a little different and the bands around the top are different colors—one has red bands, the other has black.

Metal accessories with the Red Poppy decal are relatively abundant. Many were available through Montgomery Ward mail order catalogs in the 1940's. Metal pieces are subject to dents through abuse and damage to their enamel finish from improper cleaning. Most collectors are still resisting the temptation to buy metal items which are in poor condition. Three different styles of bread boxes have been reported. None of these is easy to find. Other hard-to-find items include the dustpan and soap dispenser.

Reports of a waffle iron produced in the Red Poppy pattern always seem to lead to a decal which is similar to and goes well with Hall's Red Poppy decal. This decal has red poppy-like flowers which are much smaller than the ones on Hall pieces. Also, the stem of the flower on the waffle iron has both black and green leaves. The Hall Red Poppy decal has only black leaves. The waffle iron has a metal base and metal lid which contains the decaled china insert. The back of the waffle iron is marked "SAMSON NO. E128; Samson United Corp., Rochester, NY." A dinnerware set with this decal exists. The set was made by AVCO China Co. of Alliance, Ohio.

Glass Accessories	Price
Canister, gallon	20.00-22.00
Tumbler, clear	16.00-18.00
Tumbler, frosted, 2 styles	10.00-12.00

Metal Accessories	Price
Bread box, three styles	20.00-25.00
Cake safe	18.00-20.00
Canister set, round 5 pc.	25.00-30.00
Canister set, square 4 pc.	30.00-35.00
Clock, metal teapot shape	40.00-45.00
Coffee dispenser	18.00-20.00
Dust pan	22.00-25.00
Hot pad	8.00-10.00
Match safe	25.00-30.00
Recipe box	18.00-22.00
Shakers, ea.	4.00-6.00
Sifter	16.00-18.00
Soap dispenser	25.00-30.00

Metal Accessories	Price
Tray, rectangular	18.00-20.00
Tray, round	16.00-18.00
Waste can, 12½" oval	22.00-25.00
Waste can, round	22.00-27.00
Waste can, step-on	30.00-35.00
Waxed paper dispenser	25.00-30.00

Plastic Accessories	Price
Bowl covers, 8 pc. set	35.00-40.00
Clock, teapot shape	35.00-40.00
Mixer cover	12.00-14.00
Toaster cover	12.00-14.00

Miscellaneous Accessories	Price
Cutting board, wooden	25.00-30.00
Silverware box, wooden	35.00-40.00
Tablecloth, cotton	45.00-55.00

Row 1: Cutting board; coffee dispenser; sifter. **Row 2:** Canister set, square; shaker, round metal; hotpad. **Row 3:** Canister set, round; matchholder. **Row 4:** Waxed paper dispenser; tablecloth; recipe box. **Row 5:** Tray, round; tray, rectangular.

Row 1: Shakers, teardrop; creamer, modern; gravy boat; tumblers, 10 oz. frosted. **Row 2:** Cup and saucer (pattern outside); cup and saucer (pattern inside); bowl, 9″ salad; bowl, 9″ round. **Row 3:** Pie baker; cake plate; bowl, 8½″ flat soup. **Row 4:** Plate, 6″; plate, 7″; plate, 9″. **Row 5:** Platter, 13¼″; bowl, 6″ cereal; bowl, 5½″ fruit.

Serenade

The autumn-colored floral Serenade pattern was made for the Eureka Tea Company of Chicago. The complete D-style dinnerware is available, although most pieces are not easy to find. A growing list of kitchenware pieces has sparked collectors' interest.

Basic kitchenware items such as mixing bowls, bakers, casseroles and handled shakers are found frequently. Hard-to-find items include the pretzel jar, New York teapot, New England bean pot and the all-china drip coffee pot.

Collectors should be aware this decal will also appear on china produced by companies other than Hall.

Row 1: Drip coffee pot, "Kadota"; casserole, "Radiance." **Row 2:** Sugar and creamer, modern; shaker, handled; Bowl, 6″ "Radiance."

Row 1: Drip coffee, "Kadota"; jug, "Simplicity." **Row 2:** Beverage mug; shakers, "Five Band"; salt, "Medallion"; drip jar, "Medallion"; pepper, "Medallion."

Other Accessories	Price
Bread box	65.00-75.00
Cake safe	25.00-30.00
Canister, one-gallon glass with green decal	18.00-20.00
Canister set, 4 pc. metal	35.00-40.00
Clock, electric	60.00-65.00
Coffee dispenser	25.00-30.00
Coaster	3.00-4.00
Double boiler, enamel	30.00-32.00
Kitchen utensils, wooden handled, ea.	10.00-12.00
Match safe	20.00-25.00
Metal tray, oval	25.00-28.00
Metal tray, rectangular	20.00-22.00
Mirror	65.00-75.00
Pitcher, crystal, Federal	85.00-95.00
Pitcher, crystal, MacBeth-Evans style	95.00-110.00
Rolling pin, china (not Hall)	55.00-65.00
Sifter	25.00-30.00
Soap dispenser	30.00-35.00
Shakers, large metal, ea.	10.00-12.00
Shelf paper (30 ft. pack)	40.00-50.00
Silverware box	50.00-60.00
Tumbler, 10 oz., crystal	15.00-18.00
Waffle iron	65.00-75.00
Waste basket	25.00-30.00
Waxed paper dispenser	30.00-35.00

Springtime

The Springtime decal consists of a floral sprig with a prominent grayish-white flower accented by numerous smaller red and yellow flowers. All pieces in the pattern are also trimmed with a silver band. The dinnerware line is comprised of the entire number of D-style items. However, some pieces of dinnerware appear to be eluding the efforts of some collectors to obtain them within a reasonable amount of time.

Some of the Springtime kitchenware items appear on the market quite frequently. Among these are the cake plate, covered drip jar, ball jug and the casserole. The all-china drip coffee pot is the hardest item to locate—and probably the most expensive.

D-style Dinnerware	Price
Bowl, 5½″ fruit	2.50-3.50
Bowl, 6″ cereal	4.00-6.00
Bowl, 8½″ flat soup	7.00-9.00
Bowl, 9¼″ round	12.00-14.00
Bowl, oval	12.00-14.00
Cup	4.00-5.50
Gravy boat	16.00-18.00
Plate, 6″	2.00-3.00
Plate, 7¼″	3.00-4.00
Plate, 8¼″	3.00-4.00
Plate, 9″	4.50-5.50
Platter, 11¼″ oval	10.00-12.00
Platter, 13¼″ oval	12.00-14.00
Platter, 15″ oval	16.00-18.00
Saucer	1.00-1.50

Kitchenware	Price
Ball jug #3	18.00-22.00
Bowl, 9″ salad	10.00-12.00
Bowl, 6″ "Thick Rim"	6.00-8.00
Bowl, 7½″ "Thick Rim"	8.00-10.00
Bowl, 8½″ "Thick Rim"	10.00-12.00
Cakeplate	10.00-12.00
Casserole, "Thick Rim"	18.00-22.00
Creamer, modern	5.00-6.00
Coffee pot, Washington	22.00-30.00
Custard	3.50-4.00
Drip coffee pot, "Kadota" all-china	50.00-60.00
Drip jar and cover, "Thick Rim"	14.00-16.00
Jug, #6 "Radiance"	18.00-20.00
Pie baker	12.00-14.00
Shakers, handled, ea.	7.00-9.00
Sugar and lid, modern	8.00-9.00
Teapot, French	30.00-35.00

Row 1: Ball jug #3; teapot, French; shaker, handled; bowl, 5½″ fruit. **Row 2:** Casserole, "Thick Rim"; cake plate, cup and saucer.

Tulip

The Tulip decal is a budding lavendar and pink floral representation on an ivory body with platinum trim. This pattern was used as a premium by the Cook Coffee Company. The dinnerware shape is D-style with the addition of a 10″ dinner plate and the omission of the 8¼″ plate. Other potteries such as Harker and Paden City also used this same decal on some of their wares.

The "Perk" coffee pot pictured on the top row and the "Kadota" all-china drip coffee pot both have the Drip-O-lator backstamp of Enterprise Aluminum Company. The "Perk coffee pot will also be found in colored glazes without a decal, but this is the only decal line in which this shape pot has been found.

Collectors seem to be having the most trouble finding the "Radiance" stack set and the St. Denis cups and saucers. Obtaining Hall dinnerware also seems to be more difficult than finding Harker dinnerware. Although there are numerous Hall shapes to collect in this pattern, many collectors are mixing in pieces made by other companies. The rolling pin and pie server made by Harker are especially desirable.

D-style Dinnerware	Price
Bowl, 5½″ fruit	3.50-4.00
Bowl, 6″ cereal	5.00-7.00
Bowl, 8½″ flat soup	7.00-9.00
Bowl, 9¼″ round	14.00-17.00
Bowl, oval	12.00-15.00
Cup	4.00-5.00
Gravy boat	18.00-20.00
Plate, 6″	3.00-4.00
Plate, 7″	4.00-5.00
Plate, 9″	4.00-6.00
Plate, 10″	6.00-8.00
Platter, 11¼″	12.00-14.00
Platter, 13¼″	14.00-16.00
Saucer	1.00-1.50

Kitchenware	Price
Baker, French fluted	14.00-17.00
Bowl, 9″ salad	12.00-14.00
Bowl, 6″ "Radiance"	7.00-9.00
Bowl, 7½″ "Radiance"	10.00-12.00
Bowl, 9″ "Radiance"	12.00-14.00
Bowl, 6″ "Thick Rim"	8.00-10.00
Bowl, 7½″ "Thick Rim"	12.00-14.00
Bowl, 8½″ "Thick Rim"	15.00-17.00
Casserole, "Radiance"	25.00-30.00
Casserole, "Thick Rim"	25.00-30.00
Coffee pot, "Perk"	30.00-35.00
Creamer, modern	6.00-8.00
Cup, St. Denis	14.00-16.00
Custard	3.50-4.50
Drip coffe pot, "Kadota" all-china	55.00-65.00
Drip jar and cover, "Thick Rim"	14.00-16.00
Saucer, St. Denis	4.00-5.00
Shaker, handled, ea.	8.00-9.00
Stack set, "Radiance"	50.00-55.00
Sugar and lid, modern	10.00-12.00

Row 1: Coffee pot, "Perk"; shakers, handled. **Row 2:** Creamer and sugar, modern; cup and saucer. **Row 3:** Bowl, 9″ round; bowl, 9″ "Radiance." **Row 4:** Plate, 6″; plate, 9″. **Row 5:** Platter, 13¼″ oval; baker French.

Wildfire

The Wildfire pattern was used as a premium by the Great American Tea Company during the 1950's. The dinnerware is D-style, but the 8¼" salad plate and an oval bowl were added.

Notice the sunken handle "Thick Rim" casserole with the cadet base. The base does not have the Wildfire pattern and is interchangeable with those of other patterns such as Royal Rose and Morning Glory. Sets of utility bowls in both the straight sided and "Thick Rim" styles have been found with cadet exteriors and white interiors.

On these bowls the decal is on the inside, whereas it is on the outside of the regular white bowls.

Two styles of Aladdin teapots with the Wildfire decal have been reported—round opening and oval opening. Infusors may be obtained for both styles. The S-lid coffee pot has been found with an electric heating element and glass dripper. An example is shown on the top row. Rarely found pieces include the egg cup, "Pert" shakers, "Pert" jug, "Pert" teapot and Boston teapot.

D-style Dinnerware	Price
Bowl, 5½" fruit	3.00-3.50
Bowl, 6" cereal	5.00-6.50
Bowl, 8½" flat soup	9.00-10.00
Bowl, 9¼" round	14.00-16.00
Bowl, oval	12.00-14.00
Cup	4.00-5.00
Gravy boat	15.00-18.00
Plate, 6"	2.00-2.50
Plate, 7"	3.50-4.00
Plate, 9"	4.00-5.00
Plate, 10"	6.00-8.00
Platter, 11¼"	10.00-12.00
Platter, 13¼"	12.00-15.00
Saucer	1.00-1.50
Tidbit, 3-tier	25.00-30.00

Kitchenware	Price
Baker, French fluted	12.00-14.00
Bowl, 9" salad	10.00-12.00
Bowl, 6" straight-sided	7.00-9.00
Bowl, 7½" straight-sided	8.00-10.00
Bowl, 9" straight-sided	10.00-12.00
Bowl, 6" "Thick Rim"	9.00-11.00
Bowl, 7½" "Thick Rim"	12.00-14.00
Bowl, 8½" "Thick Rim"	16.00-18.00

Kitchenware	Price
Cakeplate	10.00-12.00
Casserole, tab-handled	20.00-22.00
Casserole, "Thick Rim"	20.00-22.00
Coffee pot, S-lid	30.00-35.00
Coffee pot, S-lid (glass dripper)	55.00-65.00
Creamer, modern	7.00-9.00
Creamer, "Pert"	8.00-10.00
Custard	4.00-5.00
Drip jar, tab-handled	12.00-14.00
Drip jar and cover, "Thick Rim"	12.00-14.00
Egg cup	35.00-40.00
Jug, 5" "Pert"	25.00-30.00
Jug, #5 "Radiance"	22.00-27.00
Pie baker	14.00-16.00
Shakers, handled, ea.	7.00-8.50
Shakers, "Pert," ea.	10.00-12.00
Shakers, teardrop, ea.	5.00-6.00
Sugar and lid, modern	10.00-12.00
Sugar, "Pert"	8.00-10.00
Teapot, Aladdin	32.00-37.00
Teapot, Boston	65.00-75.00
Teapot, 6-cup "Pert"	55.00-65.00

Metal Accessories	
Coffee dispenser	10.00-12.00

Row 1: Coffee pot, S-lid with glass dripper; shakers, teardrop style; teapot, Aladdin. **Row 2:** Bowl, 9″ salad; bowl, 9″ round; bowl, 8½″ flat soup. **Row 3:** Sugar and creamer, "Pert"; casserole, "Thick Rim"; custard, straight-sided; shaker, handled. **Row 4:** tidbit, 3-tier; plate, 7¼″; plate, 10″.

Yellow Rose

Yellow Rose was produced for the Eureka Tea Company of Chicago. Distribution of this pattern was regional and collectors are having very little success finding any outside of the northern midwest area.

The "Norse" shape teapot, sugar and creamer are found frequently in this pattern, but this shape has not been found in other decal lines. Finding the "Radiance" stack set and the all-china drip coffee is proving to be a challenge for collectors.

D-style Dinnerware	Price
Bowl, 5½" fruit	3.00-3.50
Bowl, 6" cereal	4.00-5.00
Bowl, 8½" flat soup	8.00-9.00
Bowl, 9¼" round vegetable	12.00-14.00
Cup	4.00-5.00
Gravy boat	18.00-20.00
Plate, 6"	1.50-2.50
Plate, 8¼"	3.50-4.00
Plate, 9"	4.00-6.00
Platter, 11¼" oval	10.00-12.00
Platter, 13¼" oval	12.00-14.00
Saucer	1.50-2.00

Kitchenware	
Baker, French fluted	12.00-14.00
Bowl, 9" salad	10.00-12.00
Bowl, 6" "Radiance"	6.00-8.00
Bowl, 7½" "Radiance"	8.00-10.00
Bowl, 9" "Radiance"	10.00-12.00
Casserole, "Radiance"	22.00-25.00
Coffee pot, "Dome"	22.00-27.00
Coffee pot, "Norse"	35.00-40.00
Coffee pot, "Waverly"	25.00-30.00
Creamer, "Norse"	8.00-10.00
Custard	3.00-5.00
Drip coffee pot, all-china	75.00-85.00
Drip jar and cover, "Radiance"	14.00-16.00
Onion soup	22.00-25.00
Shakers, handled, ea.	9.00-11.00
Stack set, "Radiance"	50.00-55.00
Sugar and lid, "Norse"	10.00-12.00
Teapot, New York	32.00-37.00

Row 1: Drip coffee, "Norse"; teapot, New York; creamer and sugar, "Norse." **Row 2:** Salt, handled; drip jar or covered onion soup; pepper, handled; platter, 11¼″ oval. **Row 3:** Bowl, 6″ cereal; bowl, 5½″ fruit; bowl, 8½″ flat soup. **Row 4:** Plate, 9″ dinner; plate 8¼″; cup.

Cameo Rose

Cameo Rose is an E-style dinnerware pattern which was made exclusively for the Jewel Tea Company. According to their catalog, the pattern "features a single rose, framed by a rosebud and leaf wreathe, accented in gold." It was lauded as a "superior quality hand-fired semi-porcelain dinnerware that would never fade or craze." Cameo Rose was first offered in the 1950's and remained available until the early 1970's.

Services were offered as a 16 piece "breakfast starter set," a 16 piece "dinner starter set," and a "53 piece service for eight." Individual pieces could also be bought from open stock.

Today most pieces of Cameo Rose can be found readily. However, a few items require diligent searching. The piece we have found to be the hardest to acquire is the cream soup. This is followed by the 15½" oval platter and the butter. These last two pieces were not made for the entire length of time and this may explain their scarcity.

Several other rare pieces have been reportedly purchased from a former Jewel employee. These were probably one-of-a-kind sample items which found their way to the employee's home through the employee store. These items include a wings style butter dish which is shaped like the wings butter in the Autumn Leaf pattern and a clock fashioned from a dinner plate. There is also a covered round vegetable bowl with tab handles on both the base and the lid.

Cameo Rose	Price
Bowl, 5¼" fruit	3.00-3.50
Bowl, 6¼" tab-handle cereal	3.50-4.50
Bowl, 5" cream soup	10.00-12.00
Bowl, 8" flat soup	7.00-9.00
Bowl, covered vegetable	28.00-30.00
Bowl, 9" round vegetable	12.00-14.00
Bowl, 10½" oval	12.00-14.00
Butter, ¼#	35.00-40.00
Creamer	6.00-8.00
Cup	4.50-5.00
Gravy boat and underplate	18.00-22.00
Plate, 6½"	2.50-3.00
Plate, 7¼"	3.00-4.00
Plate, 8"	4.00-5.00
Plate, 9¼"	4.00-5.00
Plate, 10"	5.00-7.00
Platter, 11¼" oval	12.00-14.00
Platter, 13¼" oval	12.00-14.00
Platter, 15½" oval	18.00-20.00
Saucer	1.00-5.00
Shakers, pr.	14.00-16.00
Sugar and lid	12.00-14.00
Teapot, 8-cup	35.00-40.00
Tidbit tray, 3-tier	27.00-32.00

Row 1: Sugar; creamer; ¼# butter; shakers. **Row 2:** Teapot; bowl, covered vegetable. **Row 3:** Cup and saucer; bowl, 5¼″ fruit; plate, 6½″. **Row 4:** Plate, 7¼″; plate, 10″.

Heather Rose

The Heather Rose decal dinnerware uses the same E-style blanks used for the Granitetone dinnerware which Hall produced for Sears starting in the 1940's. The decal is a pink rose with green leaves which are interspersed with delicate white baby's breath. Although this dinnerware pattern dates to the 1950's and 1960's, it is not plentiful. However, most pieces can be found with diligent searching. Cream soups could exist, but we have not seen any and the E-style covered vegetable bowl is not plentiful. If the E-style teapot exists, we know of several advanced collectors who would love to own it.

Several shapes, other than E-style, will be found sporting this decal. These include the New York teapot, the Irish coffee mug, the Washington coffee pot, the "Rayed" jug, the "Terrace" coffee pot, and several Flare-shape items. The New York teapot with the Heather decal is probably hard enough to find that it should be considered rare. The Washington coffee pots are of recent vintage and

still may be made on occasion if Hall desires. Two sizes are commonly found. The smaller 12 ounce size can be found with either a knob lid or a sunken lid. The larger six-cup coffee pot has only been found with the knob-style lid. The Irish coffee mug is also a newer piece, but we have not seen many. Another new piece is the small open teapot which is Hall's London shape. The "Rayed" jug is one of the more common Heather Rose pieces.

Flare-shape pieces do not appear to be common, but there are probably enough of these out there to satisfy the demand. Three sizes of bowls, a teapot and a cookie jar have been found. Other Flare-shape pieces with this decal should exist.

Some dealers and collectors are confusing this pattern with a similar Hall pattern—Primrose. Both patterns utilize the same E-style shape and a very similar rose decal, but Primrose does not have the dainty white sprigs of baby's breath.

Heather Rose	Price
Bowl, 5¼" fruit	2.50-3.00
Bowl, 6¼" cereal	3.50-4.00
Bowl, 8" flat soup	5.00-7.00
Bowl, 9" salad	9.00-11.00
Bowl, 9¼" oval	9.00-11.00
Bowl, 6¾" Flare-shape	6.00-8.00
Bowl, 7¾" Flare-shape	8.00-10.00
Bowl, 8¾" Flare-shape	9.00-11.00
Bowl, covered vegetable	15.00-18.00
Cake plate	10.00-12.00
Coffee pot, "Terrace"	28.00-30.00
Coffee pot, 30 oz. Washington	20.00-25.00
Coffee pot, 12 oz. Washington	18.00-20.00
Cookie jar, Flare-shape	20.00-25.00
Creamer	4.00-5.00
Cup	3.50-4.50
Gravy boat and underplate	12.00-14.00

Heather Rose	Price
Jug, "Rayed"	10.00-12.00
Mug, Irish coffee	12.00-14.00
Pickle dish, 9"	6.00-8.00
Pie baker	12.00-14.00
Plate, 6½"	1.50-2.00
Plate, 7¼"	3.00-3.50
Plate, 9¼"	4.00-4.50
Plate, 10"	4.50-5.50
Platter, 11¼" oval	8.00-10.00
Platter, 13¼" oval	10.00-12.00
Platter, 15½" oval	12.00-15.00
Saucer	1.00-1.50
Sugar and lid	8.00-10.00
Teapot, Flare-shape	20.00-25.00
Teapot, London	16.00-20.00
Teapot, New York	28.00-32.00

Row 1: Coffee pot, ''Terrace''; teapot, New York; coffee pot, 30 oz. Washington. **Row 2:** Bowl, covered vegetable; mug, Irish coffee; teapot, London; bowl, Flareware style.

Row 1: Bowl, tab handled cereal; bowl, oval; plate, 6″. **Row 2:** Bowl, 5¼″ fruit; gravy boat and underplate; cup and saucer.

Primrose

Primrose is an E-style dinnerware line with a floral rose decal very similar to that of Heather Rose. However, Primrose lacks the sprigs of baby's breath. Primrose was made for Grand Union during the 1950's and early 1960's.

In addition to the regular E-style dinnerware, a cakeplate, pie baker and "Rayed" jug have been found. Other pieces will probably surface eventually.

Row 1: Creamer; pie baker. Row 2: Cake plate; bowl, oval.

Primrose backstamp.

Primrose	Price
Bowl, 5¼" fruit	2.00-2.50
Bowl, 6¼" cereal	3.00-4.00
Bowl, 8" flat soup	5.00-6.00
Bowl, 9¼" oval	10.00-12.00
Cake plate	10.00-12.00
Creamer	4.00-5.00
Cup	3.00-4.00
Jug, "Rayed"	8.00-10.00
Pie baker	10.00-12.00
Plate, 6½"	2.00-2.50
Plate, 7¼"	3.00-3.50
Plate, 9¼"	3.00-4.00
Plate, 10"	4.00-5.00
Platter, 13¼" oval	10.00-12.00
Saucer	1.00-1.50
Sugar and lid	6.00-8.00

Sears' Arlington

Arlington is an E-style dinnerware pattern which Hall produced for Sears during the 1950's. Currently, not much of this pattern is appearing at shows or flea markets. The pattern is characterized by a series of three parallel blue brushstrokes which alternately intersect a winding golden vine. Pieces are nicely accented with gold trim. An example of the backstamp is shown below.

Arlington backstamp.

Left to right: Creamer and sugar; bowl, covered vegetable.

Arlington Dinnerware	Price	Arlington Dinnerware	Price
Bowl, 5¼″ fruit	2.00-2.50	Plate, 6½″	2.00-2.50
Bowl, 6¼″ cereal	2.50-3.50	Plate, 7¼″	3.00-3.50
Bowl, 5″ cream soup	6.00-8.00	Plate, 8″	2.50-3.50
Bowl, 8″ flat soup	5.00-6.00	Plate, 9¼″	3.00-3.50
Bowl, 9¼″ oval	10.00-12.00	Plate, 10″	4.00-5.00
Bowl, covered vegetable	15.00-18.00	Platter, 11¼″ oval	9.00-11.00
Creamer	4.00-5.00	Platter, 13¼″ oval	10.00-12.00
Cup	3.00-4.00	Platter, 15½″ oval	12.00-14.00
Gravy boat and underplate	10.00-12.00	Saucer	1.00-1.50
Pickle dish, 9″	4.00-5.00	Sugar and lid	6.00-8.00

Sears' Monticello

Monticello was introduced in 1941 as a pattern of Harmony House Granitetone dinnerware line by Sears. This pattern was discontinued in 1959. Granitetone was created for Sears by the noted designer, J. Palin Thorely. The pattern utilized Hall's E-style dinnerware and was named after Thomas Jefferson's Virginia home. According to Sears' ads, it features "flower sprigs in dainty blue, blue-green, pink and yellow colors scattered in profusion on each piece." A 32-piece service for six sold for $5.79 and was designed to provide the fine china look for a modest price.

Matching style white granitone candlesticks without the pattern could also be added to the set. These tall candles sold for $1.69 a pair.

Row 1: Bowl, flat soup; Plate, 10″ dinner. **Row 2:** Creamer and sugar; bowl, covered vegetable. **Row 3:** Bowl, 9¼″ oval; bowl, 5¼″ fruit; cup and saucer.

Monticello Dinnerware	Price
Bowl, 5¼″ fruit	2.00-2.50
Bowl, 6¼″ cereal	3.50-4.50
Bowl, 8″ flat soup	6.00-7.00
Bowl, 9¼″ oval	10.00-12.00
Bowl, covered vegetable	20.00-25.00
Creamer	4.00-5.00
Cup	3.00-4.00
Gravy boat and underplate	10.00-12.00
Pickle dish, 9″	4.00-5.00
Plate, 6½″	2.00-2.50
Plate, 8″	2.50-3.50
Plate, 9¼″	3.00-3.50
Plate, 10″	4.00-5.00
Platter, 11¼″ oval	9.00-11.00

Monticello Dinnerware	Price
Platter, 13¼″ oval	10.00-12.00
Platter, 15½″ oval	12.00-14.00
Saucer	1.00-1.50
Sugar and lid	6.00-8.00

Monticello backstamp.

Sears' Mount Vernon

The Mount Vernon pattern was sold under Sears' Harmony House label. This pattern was offered in the catalog from 1941 through 1959. The style was created by designer J. Palin Thorley and the decoration was the most exquisite of the contemporary designs which Hall produced for Sears. The plate design consists of a blue-green and tan leaf border with an inner wreath of pink roses. Edges, handles, knobs and feet are trimmed in 22K Coin Gold.

The eight-cup all-china drip coffee maker shown on the top shelf was available in this pattern from 1942 to 1948. The coffee maker and 100 paper filters sold for $2.89. Also, a three piece Hostess Set which included a creamer and covered sugar with the coffee maker could be bought for $4.65. Plain white 8½″ tall candlesticks which matched the style of the dinnerware were available for $1.69 a pair.

Row 1: Sugar and lid; Drip coffee, all-china; creamer. **Row 2:** Cup and saucer; bowl, 8½″ flat soup; bowl, 5¼″ fruit.

Mount Vernon Dinnerware	Price	Mount Vernon Dinnerware	Price
Bowl, 5¼″ fruit	2.00-2.50	Plate, 6½″	2.00-2.50
Bowl, 6¼″ cereal	3.50-4.50	Plate, 8″	2.50-3.50
Bowl, 8″ flat soup	6.00-8.00	Plate, 9¼″	3.00-3.50
Bowl, 9¼″ oval	10.00-12.00	Plate, 10″	4.00-5.00
Bowl, covered vegetable	25.00-30.00	Platter, 11¼″ oval	9.00-11.00
Coffee pot, all-china	60.00-70.00	Platter, 13¼″ oval	10.00-12.00
Creamer	4.00-5.00	Platter, 15½″ oval	12.00-14.00
Cup	3.00-4.00	Saucer	1.00-1.50
Gravy boat and underplate	10.00-12.00	Sugar and lid	6.00-8.00
Pickle dish, 9″	4.00-5.00		

Sears' Richmond/Brown-Eyed Susan

Richmond and Brown-Eyed Susan are two names for Hall dinnerware with the same decal. The decal consists of a cluster of brown, pink and yellow meadow flowers which are used as a center decoration. The beauty of the design is enhanced by the use of 22K gold trim. The Richmond design, as selected by Sears, was intended to match the floral decoration of some of the Duncan Phyfe fabric of the period. Richmond had a relatively short life with Sears. It was introduced in 1941 and disappeared from their catalog in 1946.

Later, in the 1960's, this pattern was revived by Hall under the name Brown-Eyed Susan for use by trading stamp companies. Pieces from this later issue will not bear the Harmony House backstamp. During this period, Hall also used this decal on some kitchenware shapes. These additional kitchenware items which were made will be indicated by (BES) in the listing below.

Row 1: Jug, "Rayed"; bowl, 9″ salad. **Row 2:** Cup and saucer; plate, 9¼″ dinner; bowl, 5¼″ sauce.

Richmond/Brown-Eyed Susan	Price
Baker, French flute (BES)	10.00-12.00
Bowl, 5¼″ fruit	2.00-3.00
Bowl, 6¼″ cereal	3.00-4.00
Bowl, 8″ flat soup	5.00-6.00
Bowl, 9″ salad (BES)	10.00-12.00
Bowl, 9¼″ oval	9.00-11.00
Bowl, covered vegetable	18.00-22.00
Creamer	4.00-5.00
Cup	4.00-4.50
Gravy boat and underplate	10.00-12.00
Jug, "Rayed" (BES)	10.00-12.00

Richmond/Brown-Eyed Susan	Price
Pickle dish, 9″	4.00-5.00
Plate, 6½″	2.00-2.50
Plate, 7¼″	3.00-3.50
Plate, 9¼″	3.00-4.00
Plate, 10″	4.00-5.00
Platter, 11¼″ oval	9.00-10.00
Platter, 13¼″ oval	10.00-12.00
Platter, 15½″ oval	14.00-16.00
Saucer	1.00-1.50
Sugar and lid	8.00-10.00
Teapot, Aladdin (BES)	35.00-40.00

Left to right: Teapot, Aladdin; sugar and creamer.

What you should know about Sears Dinnerware

AMERICAN SEMI-PORCELAIN Made of high quality, selected dinnerware clays. Fired (baked) at lower temperatures than true china and so is not as wear-resistant. Fewer steps needed to make it than for Granitone or China. Smooth, easy-to-clean, scratch-resistant glaze (outer coating).

EXCLUSIVE GRANITONE Superior to ordinary semi-porcelain dinnerware because—Same quality imported and American clays as True China. Fired (baked) at only slightly lower temperatures than True China; is nearly as vitrified (glass-hard throughout) as True China. Glaze (outer coating) is as hard as on True China; is more durable than glaze found on semi-porcelain.

AMERICAN TRUE CHINA. Made of finest quality china clays obtainable. Exacting care taken by skilled workers through every step makes it more expensive to make than any other type. Fired (baked) at very high temperatures so that it is fully vitrified (glass-hard throughout) and translucent (you can see the shadow of your hand through it).

Smooth glaze (glass-like outer coating) actually fused into body for outstanding durability. Crazeproof (glaze will never crack). Highly chip-resistant. Lovely decorations plus unequaled beauty and quality manufacture make it practical for every day and a possession of heirloom value.

How to choose the right size Dinnerware Set for your needs

SET COMPOSITIONS

20-piece set—place service for 4
Four each: Tea cups, Saucers, Bread and Butter Plates (6-inch), Dinner Plates (9-inch), Sauce Dishes (5¼-inch). (Extra large 9¾-inch dinner plates in True China sets.)

32-piece set—standard service for 6
Six each: Tea cups, Saucers, Bread and Butter Plates (6-inch), Dinner Plates (9-inch), Sauce Dishes (5¼-inch). One each: Small Platter (11-inch), Open Vegetable Dish.

35-piece set—complete service for 6
Same as 32-piece set above except has double-purpose 6-inch cereal-soup dishes instead of 5¼-inch sauce dishes and has Covered Sugar Bowl and Creamer.

53-piece set—service for 8
Eight each: Tea cups, Saucers, Bread and Butter Plates (6-inch), Large Dinner Plates (9¾-inch), Soup Plates, Sauce Dishes (5¼-inch). One each: Covered Sugar Bowl (2 pieces), Cream Pitcher, Medium Platter (13-inch), Open Vegetable Dish.

93-piece set—True China service for 12
Twelve each: Tea cups, Saucers, Bread and Butter Plates (6-inch), Pie Plates, Large Dinner Plates (9¾-inch), Soup Plates, Sauce Dishes (5¼-inch). One each: Covered Sugar Bowl (2 pieces), Cream Pitcher, Covered Vegetable Dish (2 pieces), Gravy Boat with attached stand, Small Platter, Large Platter, and Open Vegetable Dish.

95-piece set—service for 12
Same as 93-piece set above except Gravy Boat and Stand are separate (2 pieces), and has two Open Vegetable Dishes.

All Sears Dinnerware is packed as carefully as eggs in a crate. However, in line with our guarantee of complete satisfaction, we guarantee replacement of any piece broken in shipment. You need not hesitate to buy by mail.

OPEN STOCK AVAILABLE on all Sears dinnerware patterns as long as they are manufactured. You will be notified in plenty of time to order extra pieces before your pattern is dropped from the catalog.

BUILD YOUR OWN SET OF DINNERWARE. Maybe you need more serving dishes than we list in the set compositions. Then, order as many extra pieces from Open Stock as your dining needs require. Replace broken pieces promptly and keep your dinnerware sets complete—your table will look its best!

OPEN STOCK PRICES—American Semi-Porcelain and True China Dinnerware

Item—Approximate Sizes / State Catalog Number and Item Wanted	Shpg. Wt.	25 D 04387 ♦Springtime	35 D 04433 ♦Hemlock	35 D 04463 ♦Richmond	35 D 04464 ♦Monticello	35 D 04465 ♦Mount Vernon	35 D 04967 ♦Dorset (China)	35 D 04905 ♦Touraine / 35 D 04968 ♦Fontaine	35 D 04954 ♦Greek Key (China)
6 Tea Cups (about 7 oz.)	5 lbs.	$0.96	$1.20	$1.38	$1.56	$1.86	$3.54	$4.50	$5.34
6 Tea Saucers	5 lbs.	.66	.72	.84	.96	1.20	2.04	2.34	2.94
6 Bread and Butters, 6 in.	5 lbs.	.66	.78	.96	1.08	1.32	2.52	3.54	4.74
6 Pie or Salad Plates, 7 in.	8 lbs.	.84	.96	1.14	1.32	1.62	3.42	4.32	5.70
6 Dinner Plates, 9 inches	11 lbs.	1.14	1.44	1.68	1.98	2.34			
6 Lge. Dinner Plates, 9¾ in.	12 lbs.	1.38	1.68	1.98	2.28	2.64	5.34	5.94	7.14
6 Soup Plates, 7½ inches	9 lbs.	1.02	1.44	1.68	1.98	2.34	3.90	4.44	5.88
6 Handled Cream Soups	6 lbs.		1.62	3.66	3.96	4.62	5.70	8.34	9.90
6 Sauce Dishes, 5½ in.	5 lbs.	.60	.72	.84	.96	1.20	2.04	2.70	4.14
1 Covered Sugar Bowl	2 lbs.	.63	.78	.95	1.00	1.22	1.98	2.85	3.76
1 Cream Pitcher	2 lbs.	.35	.39	.49	.59	.71	1.29	1.84	2.19
1 Covered Vegetable Dish	4 lbs.	1.19	1.39	1.85	1.99	2.45	3.75	5.98	7.98
1 Gravy Boat	3 lbs.	.45	.54	.63	.70	.83	3.75	4.98	6.49
1 Gravy Boat Stand	1 lb.	.31	.37	.42	.55	.69			
1 Small Platter, 11 inches	4 lbs.	.36	.41	.47	.60	1.30	2.29	2.98	
1 Medium Platter, 13 inches	5 lbs.	.59	.65	.79	.90	1.15	1.89	3.39	4.49
1 Large Platter, 15 inches	6 lbs.		1.09	1.25	1.35	1.65	3.50	4.98	6.49
1 Round Open Veg. Dish	3 lbs.	.35	.45						
1 Oval Open Veg. Dish	3 lbs.			.53	.59	.70	1.19	2.39	2.99

♦ **Shipping Points**—Order Open Stock from Sears Mail Order House nearest you. You pay postage from there. Shipped from Chicago, Philadelphia or Los Angeles.

Eva Zeisel Designs

Eva Zeisel designed the Tomorrow's Classic and Century shapes which were produced by Hall China. She was essentially working as a free lance designer while she held a teaching position at Pratt Institute in the early 1950's. In 1952, nine decal patterns were created by Zeisel and her associates and students. The ensuing years resulted in the addition of more patterns. However, production problems at Hall led to the acquisition of the molds by the Hollydale Pottery of California in 1957.

The Century shape consists of a dinnerware service which includes 23 pieces. There are four different patterns—white and three decal patterns. Plates consist of slightly distended ovals which are elongated into gently arching tips which also serve as handles. Platters and bowls are slightly elongated with the upward sloping tips forming double handles. The shapes of the teapots, jugs, casseroles and other accessories are equally modernistic.

The Tomorrow's Classic shape consists of 40 different pieces which comprised a futuristic-looking dinnerware service. The pieces differ only slightly in style from that used in the Century line. Plates are slight ovals which lack any elongated tips and bowls are essentially ovals which distend to a single elongated tip which forms a handle.

Hallcraft Century backstamp.

Fern

The Hallcraft Fern pattern consists of 23 pieces of stylized china. The decal is comprised of leaf-like shapes in mulberry, green and pastel blue set on a lace-like grey background. The interiors of the jugs, cups and the tops of the casserole lids, sugar lids and teapot lids are glazed in pastel blue. Cups may be found both with the decal and without.

Hallcraft Fern	Price
Ashtray	4.00-5.00
Bowl, 5¾″ fruit	2.00-3.00
Bowl, 8″ soup	4.00-6.00
Bowl, 11¾″ salad	8.00-10.00
Bowl, 10½″ vegetable	10.00-12.00
Bowl, divided vegetable	10.00-12.00
Butter dish	20.00-25.00
Casserole	18.00-20.00
Creamer	3.00-4.00
Cup	2.50-3.50
Gravy boat	8.00-10.00
Jug	7.00-9.00

Hallcraft Fern	Price
Ladle	4.00-6.00
Plate, 6″	1.00-1.50
Plate, 8″	1.50-2.50
Plate, 10¼″	3.00-4.00
Platter, 13¾″	8.00-10.00
Platter, 15″	10.00-12.00
Relish, 4-part	10.00-12.00
Saucer	.50-1.00
Shaker, ea.	3.00-4.00
Sugar and cover	5.00-7.00
Teapot, 6-cup	20.00-25.00

Row 1: Jug; casserole. **Row 2:** Bowl, 8″ soup; bowl, 11¾″ salad. **Row 3:** Plate, 8″ salad; cup and saucer; bowl, 5¾″ fruit. **Row 4:** Bowl, divided vegetable; relish, 4-part.

Sunglow

The Sunglow pattern of the Hallcraft Century shape consists of a decal which features a thin tree dotted with brilliant yellow leaves. Randomly dispersing yellow leaves also generously adorn the otherwise stark exterior surfaces. The interiors of the jugs, cups and the tops of the casseroles, teapots and sugar lids are also finished in a matching yellow glaze. Some cups will be found with only the interior yellow glaze, while others will also sport the decal decoration.

Row 1: Plate, 8″; platter, 13¾″. **Row 2:** Bowl, divided vegetable; cup and saucer; plate, 6″.

Century Sunglow	Price	Century Sunglow	Price
Ashtray	3.00-4.00	Ladle	4.00-5.00
Bowl, 5¾″ fruit	2.00-2.50	Plate, 6″	1.00-1.50
Bowl, 8″ soup	4.00-5.00	Plate, 8″	1.50-2.50
Bowl, 11¾″ salad	7.00-9.00	Plate, 10¼″	3.00-4.00
Bowl, 10½″ vegetable	9.00-11.00	Platter, 13¾″	8.00-10.00
Bowl, divided vegetable	10.00-12.00	Platter, 15″	10.00-12.00
Butter dish	20.00-25.00	Relish, 4-part	10.00-12.00
Casserole	15.00-18.00	Saucer	.50-1.00
Creamer	3.00-4.00	Shaker, ea.	3.00-4.00
Cup	2.50-3.00	Sugar and cover	5.00-6.00
Gravy boat	8.00-10.00	Teapot, 6-cup	20.00-25.00
Jug	7.00-9.00		

Hallcraft

Ad for Hallcraft by distributor Midhurst China Company in the *China and Glass Red Book* from the mid-fifties.

Hallcraft advertising ashtray.

Arizona and Buckingham

Tomorrow's Classic Arizona pattern features a decal with rust colored leaves set against a background with traces of fine black lines. The design was originated by Charles Seliger who was an associate of Eva Zeisel. Designer Erik Blegvad was responsible for the creation of the Buckingham pattern. Pieces in this pattern exhibit a iron grillwork fence. The design varies slightly among the various items in the pattern as may be seen in the photograph. The shape of the fence is different and trees will be interspersed in some fences and lacking in others.

Row 1: Jug, 1¼ qt. Arizona; gravy boat, Arizona. **Row 2:** Teapot, Buckingham; jug, 1¼ qt. Buckingham.

Item	Arizona	Buckingham
Ashtray	3.00-4.00	4.00-5.00
Bowl, 5¾″ fruit	2.00-2.50	3.00-3.50
Bowl, 6″ cereal	2.50-3.00	3.50-4.50
Bowl, 9″ coupe soup	3.00-4.50	5.00-6.00
Bowl, 8¾″ sq. open vegetable	8.00-10.00	10.00-12.00
Bowl, 14½″ large salad	8.00-10.00	10.00-12.00
Bowl, 11 oz. open baker	7.00-9.00	9.00-11.00
Bowl, oval celery	7.00-9.00	9.00-11.00
Bowl, large ftd. fruit	10.00-12.00	12.00-15.00
Butter dish	20.00-25.00	25.00-30.00
Candlestick, 4½″	10.00-12.00	12.00-14.00
Candlestick, 8″	10.00-12.00	12.00-14.00
Casserole, 1¼ qt.	10.00-12.00	12.00-15.00
Casserole, 2 qt.	12.00-14.00	15.00-17.00
Coffee pot, 6-cup	18.00-22.00	25.00-30.00
Creamer	3.00-4.00	5.00-6.00
Creamer, A.D.	3.00-4.00	5.00-6.00
Cup	3.00-3.50	3.00-4.00
Cup, A.D.	3.00-4.00	3.50-4.50
Egg cup	10.00-12.00	15.00-18.00
Gravy boat	7.00-9.00	10.00-12.00
Jug, 1¼ qt.	7.00-9.00	10.00-12.00
Jug, 3 qt.	9.00-11.00	12.00-14.00
Ladle	4.00-5.00	6.00-8.00
Marmite and cover	10.00-12.00	12.00-14.00
Onion soup and cover	10.00-12.00	12.00-14.00
Plate, 6″	1.00-1.50	1.50-2.00
Plate, 8″	1.50-2.50	2.50-3.50
Plate, 11″	4.00-5.00	4.00-5.00
Platter, 12¼″	7.00-9.00	9.00-11.00
Platter, 15″	10.00-12.00	12.00-14.00
Platter, 17″	12.00-14.00	15.00-18.00
Saucer	.50-1.00	1.00-1.50
Saucer, A.D.	1.00-1.50	1.00-1.50
Shaker, ea.	3.00-4.00	5.00-6.00
Sugar and cover	5.00-6.00	6.00-8.00
Sugar, open A.D.	3.00-4.00	5.00-6.00
Teapot, 6-cup	20.00-25.00	25.00-30.00
Vase	10.00-12.00	12.00-14.00
Vinegar bottle	10.00-12.00	12.00-14.00

Bouquet

The colorful floral Bouquet pattern is beginning to appeal to collectors. This pattern seems to be the most readily available and the most highly collected of all the Hallcraft designs. In addition to the 40 pieces of Classic shape, col-

lectors will also find this decal on a shape designated "M.J." by some researchers. The "M.J." casserole and electric percolator are shown in the photographs.

Row 1: Shakers; ashtray; marmite; egg cup. **Row 2:** Casserole, 2 qt.; casserole, "M.J." shape; candlestick, 4½".

Bouquet	Price	Bouquet	Price
Ashtray	4.00-5.00	Gravy boat	10.00-12.00
Bowl, 5¾″ fruit	3.00-3.50	Jug, 1¼ qt.	10.00-12.00
Bowl, 6″ cereal	3.50-4.50	Jug, 3 qt.	14.00-16.00
Bowl, 9″ coupe soup	5.00-6.00	Ladle	6.00-8.00
Bowl, 8¾″ sq. open vegetable	12.00-14.00	Marmite and cover	12.00-14.00
Bowl, 14½″ large salad	12.00-14.00	Onion soup and cover	12.00-14.00
Bowl, 11 oz. open baker	9.00-11.00	Percolator, electric	45.00-55.00
Bowl, oval celery	10.00-12.00	Plate, 6″	1.50-2.00
Bowl, large ftd. fruit	18.00-20.00	Plate, 8″	2.50-3.50
Butter dish	25.00-30.00	Plate, 11″	4.00-5.00
Candlestick, 4½″	12.00-14.00	Platter, 12¼″	9.00-11.00
Candlestick, 8″	12.00-14.00	Platter, 15″	12.00-14.00
Casserole, 1¼ qt.	12.00-15.00	Platter, 17″	15.00-18.00
Casserole, 2 qt.	15.00-17.00	Saucer	1.00-1.50
Casserole, "M.J."	25.00-30.00	Saucer, A.D.	1.00-1.50
Coffee pot, 6-cup	25.00-30.00	Shaker, ea.	5.00-6.00
Creamer	5.00-6.00	Sugar and cover	6.00-8.00
Creamer, A.D.	5.00-6.00	Sugar, open A.D.	5.00-6.00
Cup	3.00-4.00	Teapot, 6-cup	25.00-30.00
Cup, A.D.	3.50-4.50	Vase	14.00-16.00
Egg Cup	18.00-20.00	Vinegar bottle	14.00-16.00

Row 1: Coffee pot; electric percolator; teapot. **Row 2:** Jug, 1¼ qt.; ladle; gravy boat; creamer and sugar. **Row 3:** Butter; sugar, A.D.; creamer, A.D.; cup and saucer. **Row 4:** Bowl, 8¾″ sq.; bowl, 9″; bowl, 5¾″ fruit. **Row 5:** Plate, 6″; platter, 15″.

Caprice

Caprice is a Tomorrow's Classic leaf and floral design. The colors are pastel pinks, greys and yellows. Discerning the pattern on some of the smaller pieces is sometimes confusing since only one part of the pattern often appears on the piece.

Caprice	Price
Ashtray	3.00-4.00
Bowl, 5¾″ fruit	2.50-3.00
Bowl, 6″ cereal	3.00-4.00
Bowl, 9″ coupe soup	5.00-6.00
Bowl, 8¾″ sq. open vegetable	10.00-12.00
Bowl, 14½″ large salad	10.00-12.00
Bowl, 11 oz. open baker	9.00-11.00
Bowl, oval celery	9.00-10.00
Bowl, large ftd. fruit	14.00-16.00
Butter dish	25.00-30.00
Candlestick, 4½″	8.00-10.00
Candlestick, 8″	12.00-14.00
Casserole, 1¼ qt.	11.00-13.00
Casserole, 2 qt.	14.00-16.00
Coffee pot, 6-cup	25.00-30.00
Creamer	3.50-4.00
Creamer, A.D.	5.00-6.00
Cup	3.00-4.00
Cup, A.D.	3.50-4.50
Egg cup	16.00-18.00
Gravy boat	10.00-12.00
Jug, 1¼ qt.	10.00-12.00
Jug, 3 qt.	14.00-16.00
Ladle	5.00-6.00
Marmite and cover	10.00-12.00
Onion soup and cover	12.00-14.00
Plate, 6″	1.50-2.00
Plate, 8″	2.50-3.50
Plate, 11″	4.00-5.00
Platter, 12¼″	9.00-11.00
Platter, 15″	12.00-14.00
Platter, 17″	14.00-16.00
Saucer	.50-1.00
Saucer, A.D.	1.00-1.50
Shaker, ea.	4.00-5.00
Sugar and cover	6.00-8.00
Sugar, open A.D.	5.00-6.00
Teapot, 6-cup	20.00-25.00
Vase	12.00-14.00
Vinegar bottle	12.00-14.00

Row 1: Teapot; jug, 3 qt.; jug, 1¼ qt. **Row 2:** Vinegar bottle; bowl, oval celery. **Row 3:** Bowl, 8¾″ sq.; bowl, 9″.

Harlequin and Holiday

The Harlequin pattern shown on this page uses a series of abstract pink, grey and black lines to produce a decoration. Notice in the photograph other shapes than those associated with Hallcraft will be found with this decoration.

The Holiday pattern, pictured on the opposite page, features an almost gaudy combination of red and black colors used to produce a leaf-like design.

Row 1: Ball jug #3; cookie jar; ladle; teapot, Thorley design. **Row 2:** Teapot; cup and saucer; candlestick, 4½"; jug.

Item	Harlequin	Holiday
Ashtray	4.00-5.00	3.00-4.00
Ball jug #3	18.00-22.00	
Bowl, 5¾″ fruit	3.00-3.50	2.00-2.50
Bowl, 6″ cereal	3.50-4.00	2.50-3.00
Bowl, 9″ coupe soup	5.00-5.50	3.00-4.00
Bowl, 8¾″ sq. open vegetable	10.00-12.00	8.00-10.00
Bowl, 14½″ large salad	10.00-12.00	8.00-10.00
Bowl, 11 oz. open baker	7.00-9.00	7.00-9.00
Bowl, oval celery	7.00-9.00	7.00-9.00
Bowl, large ftd. fruit	12.00-15.00	10.00-12.00
Butter dish	20.00-25.00	20.00-25.00
Candlestick, 4½″	10.00-12.00	8.00-10.00
Candlestick, 8″	10.00-12.00	8.00-10.00
Casserole, 1¼ qt.	10.00-12.00	8.00-10.00
Casserole, 2 qt.	12.00-14.00	12.00-14.00
Coffee pot, 6-cup	18.00-22.00	18.00-20.00
Cookie jar	25.00-30.00	
Creamer	3.00-4.00	3.00-4.00
Creamer, A.D.	5.00-6.00	5.00-6.00
Cup	3.00-4.00	3.00-4.00
Cup, A.D.	4.00-5.00	4.00-4.50
Egg cup	12.00-15.00	12.00-15.00
Gravy boat	10.00-12.00	10.00-12.00
Jug, 1¼ qt.	8.00-10.00	8.00-10.00
Jug, 3 qt.	12.00-14.00	12.00-14.00

Item	Harlequin	Holiday
Ladle	4.00-5.00	4.00-5.00
Marmite and cover	12.00-14.00	10.00-12.00
Onion soup and cover	12.00-14.00	10.00-12.00
Plate, 6″	1.50-2.00	1.00-1.50
Plate, 8″	2.50-3.00	2.00-3.00
Plate, 11″	4.00-5.00	4.00-5.00
Platter, 12¼″	9.00-11.00	9.00-11.00
Platter, 15″	12.00-14.00	12.00-14.00
Platter, 17″	15.00-18.00	14.00-16.00
Saucer	1.00-1.50	.50-1.00
Saucer, A.D.	1.00-1.50	1.00-1.50
Shaker, ea.	3.00-4.00	3.00-4.00
Sugar and cover	6.00-8.00	6.00-8.00
Sugar, open A.D.	4.00-5.00	4.00-5.00
Teapot, 6-cup	22.00-27.00	22.00-25.00
Teapot, Thorley	45.00-55.00	
Vase	12.00-14.00	12.00-14.00
Vinegar bottle	10.00-12.00	10.00-12.00

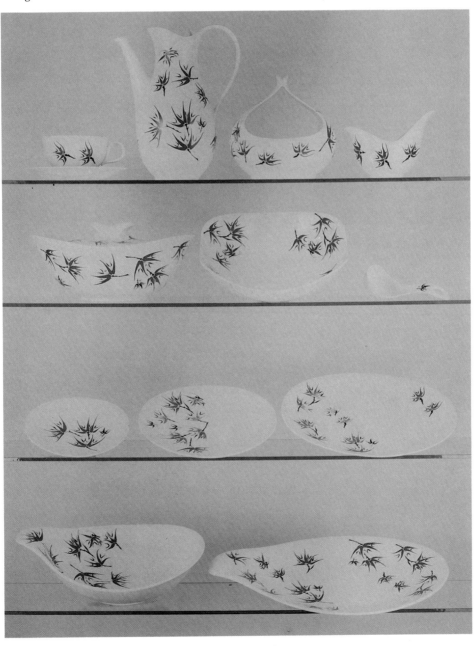

Row 1: Cup and saucer; coffee pot; gravy boat; creamer, A.D. **Row 2:** Casserole; bowl, 8¾″ sq.; ladle. **Row 3:** Plate, 6″; Plate, 8″; Plate, 11″. **Row 4:** Bowl, 9″; platter, 12¼″.

Row 1: Shakers; creamer; sugar and lid. **Row 2:** Gravy boat; ladle; cup and saucer. **Row 3:** Platter, 12¼″; bowl, 9″. **Row 4:** Bowl, oval celery; bowl, 5¾″ fruit. **Row 5:** Plate, 11″; plate, 8″; plate, 6″.

Mulberry and Peach Blossom

The Hallcraft Mulberry pattern is shown in the photograph on the opposite page. This decal consists of a branch with green leaves which is laden with purple mulberries.

The Peach Blossom decal is shown below. It is a branch-like decal which has green leaves and pastel pink flowers and flower buds. Shapes other than Hallcraft have been found with this decal. An example is the E-style oval bowl shown in this picture.

Row 1: Teapot; jug, 1¼ qt.; vinegar bottle; shakers. **Row 2:** Bowl, oval; sugar and lid; creamer; butter dish.

Item	Mulberry	Peach Blossom	Item	Mulberry	Peach Blossom
Ashtray	3.00-4.00	4.00-5.00	Gravy boat	7.00-9.00	10.00-12.00
Bowl, 5¾" fruit	2.00-2.50	3.00-3.50	Jug, 1¼ qt.	7.00-9.00	10.00-12.00
Bowl, 6" cereal	2.50-3.00	3.50-4.50	Jug, 3 qt.	9.00-11.00	12.00-14.00
Bowl, 9" coupe soup	3.00-4.50	5.00-6.00	Ladle	4.00-5.00	6.00-8.00
Bowl, 8¾" sq. open vegetable	8.00-10.00	10.00-12.00	Marmite and cover	10.00-12.00	12.00-14.00
Bowl, 14½" large salad	8.00-10.00	10.00-12.00	Onion soup and cover	10.00-12.00	12.00-14.00
Bowl, 11 oz. open baker	7.00-9.00	9.00-11.00	Plate, 6"	1.00-1.50	1.50-2.00
Bowl, oval celery	7.00-9.00	9.00-11.00	Plate, 8"	1.50-2.50	2.50-3.50
Bowl, oval E-shape		12.00-15.00	Plate, 11"	4.00-4.00	4.00-5.00
Bowl, large ftd. fruit	10.00-12.00	12.00-15.00	Platter, 12¼"	7.00-9.00	9.00-11.00
Butter dish	20.00-25.00	25.00-30.00	Platter, 15"	10.00-12.00	12.00-14.00
Candlestick, 4½"	10.00-12.00	12.00-14.00	Platter, 17"	12.00-14.00	15.00-18.00
Candlestick, 8"	10.00-12.00	12.00-14.00	Saucer	.50-1.00	1.00-1.50
Casserole, 1¼ qt.	10.00-12.00	12.00-15.00	Saucer, A.D.	1.00-1.50	1.00-1.50
Casserole, 2 qt.	12.00-14.00	15.00-17.00	Shaker, ea.	3.00-4.00	5.00-6.00
Coffee pot, 6-cup	18.00-22.00	25.00-30.00	Sugar and cover	5.00-6.00	6.00-8.00
Creamer	3.00-4.00	5.00-6.00	Sugar, open A.D.	3.00-4.00	5.00-6.00
Creamer, A.D.	3.00-4.00	5.00-6.00	Teapot, 6-cup	20.00-25.00	25.00-30.00
Cup	3.00-3.50	3.00-4.00	Vase	10.00-12.00	12.00-14.00
Cup, A.D.	3.00-4.00	3.50-4.50	Vinegar bottle	10.00-12.00	12.00-14.00
Egg cup	10.00-12.00	15.00-18.00			

Pinecone

Pinecone E-style dinnerware was produced for Grand Union during the 1950's. In addition, the decal was also used on Hallcraft Classic shape pieces. It is not known whether all the items in the Hallcraft shape were produced. Therefore, the following listing will only include the Pinecone pieces which we have seen.

Row 1: Teapot; platter, 12¼". **Row 2:** Casserole; marmite; gravy boat.

Pinecone E-style Dinnerware	Price
Bowl, 5¼" fruit	2.50-3.50
Bowl, 9" round	10.00-12.00
Cup	3.00-4.00
Plate, 6"	1.50-2.00
Plate, 7¼"	2.50-3.00
Plate, 9¼"	3.50-4.50
Saucer	1.00-1.50
Tidbit, 3-tier	18.00-20.00

Pinecone Tomorrow's Classic	Price
Ashtray	3.00-4.00
Bowl, 5¾" fruit	3.00-4.00
Bowl, 9" coupe soup	5.00-6.00
Bowl, 8¾" sq. open vegetable	10.00-12.00
Bowl, 14½" large salad	10.00-12.00
Bowl, oval celery	9.00-10.00
Butter dish	25.00-30.00
Casserole, 1¼ qt.	11.00-13.00

Pinecone Tomorrow's Classic	Price
Casserole, 2 qt.	14.00-16.00
Creamer	3.50-4.00
Cup	3.00-4.00
Gravy boat	10.00-12.00
Jug, 1¼ qt.	10.00-12.00
Jug, 3 qt.	14.00-16.00
Ladle	5.00-6.00
Marmite and cover	10.00-12.00
Onion soup and cover	12.00-14.00
Plate, 6"	1.50-2.00
Plate, 8"	2.50-3.50
Plate, 11"	4.00-5.00
Platter, 12¼"	9.00-11.00
Platter, 15"	12.00-14.00
Saucer	.50-1.00
Shaker, ea.	4.00-5.00
Sugar and cover	6.00-8.00
Teapot, 6-cup	20.00-25.00

Spring

Tomorrow's Classic Spring pattern features a pastel color floral arrangement. Pink, turquoise and green are deftly interwoven to provide a soft pleasing pattern.

Row 1: Jug; sugar, A.D.; creamer, A.D.; ashtray. **Row 2:** Butter dish; cup and saucer; plate, 6″. **Row 3:** Bowl, 9″; bowl, oval celery.

Spring	Price	Spring	Price
Ashtray	3.00-4.00	Gravy boat	10.00-12.00
Bowl, 5¾″ fruit	2.50-3.00	Jug, 1¼ qt.	10.00-12.00
Bowl, 6″ cereal	3.00-4.00	Jug, 3 qt.	14.00-16.00
Bowl, 9″ coupe soup	5.00-6.00	Ladle	5.00-6.00
Bowl, 8¾″ sq. open vegetable	10.00-12.00	Marmite and cover	10.00-12.00
Bowl, 14½″ large salad	10.00-12.00	Onion soup and cover	12.00-14.00
Bowl, 11 oz. open baker	9.00-11.00	Plate, 6″	1.50-2.00
Bowl, oval celery	9.00-10.00	Plate, 8″	2.50-3.50
Bowl, large ftd. fruit	14.00-16.00	Plate, 11″	4.00-5.00
Butter dish	25.00-30.00	Platter, 12¼″	9.00-11.00
Candlestick, 4½″	8.00-10.00	Platter, 15″	12.00-14.00
Candlestick, 8″	12.00-14.00	Platter, 17″	14.00-16.00
Casserole, 1¼ qt.	11.00-13.00	Saucer	.50-1.00
Casserole, 2 qt.	14.00-16.00	Saucer, A.D.	1.00-1.50
Coffee pot, 6-cup	25.00-30.00	Shaker, ea.	4.00-5.00
Creamer	3.50-4.00	Sugar and cover	6.00-8.00
Creamer, A.D.	5.00-6.00	Sugar, open A.D.	5.00-6.00
Cup	3.00-4.00	Teapot, 6-cup	20.00-25.00
Cup, A.D.	3.50-4.50	Vase	12.00-14.00
Egg cup	16.00-18.00	Vinegar bottle	12.00-14.00

Part II: Kitchenware

Hall introduced its first modern era kitchenware line–"Medallion"–in 1932. The two initial colors were ivory and lettuce. Successful marketing in this venture soon led to the addition of other colors and the introduction of new shapes. Decals were also applied to both ivory and cobalt bodies and new patterns of kitchenware were developed. In addition to creating new kitchenware patterns, the kitchenware shapes were decorated with the appropriate decals and were incorporated into the dinnerware lines shown in Part I.

The collectibility of the solid color kitchenware has increased remarkably over the past few years since many collectors have learned that Hall kitchenware is very serviceable as well as attractive. The Chinese red and cobalt colors have been especially popular.

The kitchenware section of this book is divided into two separate parts–kitchenware shapes and kitchenware decal designs. Patterns in each area will appear in alphabetical order.

Three "Medallion" shape reamers are shown in the photo below. Although none is common, the one in the lettuce green color is seen most often. The other two are hard enough to find that they might be considered rare. For information on pricing see the "Medallion" and "Stonewall" sections in this kitchenware chapter.

"Medallion" shape reamers.

Instructions and guarantee from Jewel pamphlet.

"Five Band"

The "Five Band" kitchenware line was introduced in 1936. Chinese red was the most popular color then and is still the most collectible color today. Other colors including cobalt, Indian red, marine, cadet, ivory and canary are often found. Some items in the "Five Band" shape will also be found decorated with numerous decals in both dinnerware and kitchenware patterns. To date the carafe has not been found with a decal. The casserole has two different types of lids–knob handle and loop-shaped handle.

Row 1: Cookie jar; carafe; syrup; shakers. **Row 2:** Bowl, 6″; jug, 6¼″; jug, 5″; batter bowl.

Item	Red/Cobalt	Other Colors
Batter bowl	40.00-50.00	15.00-18.00
Bowl, 6″	6.00-8.00	4.00-5.00
Bowl, 7¼″	8.00-10.00	4.00-5.00
Bowl, 8¾″	10.00-12.00	8.00-10.00
Carafe	65.00-70.00	40.00-50.00
Casserole, 8″	25.00-30.00	15.00-20.00
Coffee pot	35.00-40.00	16.00-18.00
Cookie jar	32.00-37.00	16.00-20.00
Jug, 6¼″	18.00-22.00	12.00-14.00
Jug, 5″	14.00-16.00	8.00-10.00
Shakers, ea.	8.00-10.00	6.00-8.00
Syrup	35.00-40.00	20.00-25.00

"Medallion"

"Medallion," which was introduced in 1932, was Hall's first kitchenware line. The original issue consisted of the square leftover, the teapot, the casserole, the four sizes of jugs and the six piece bowl set. These were made initially in the ivory and lettuce colors. Later other colors and pieces were added, but the only other color appearing with any frequency is Chinese red. Unusual pieces include the all-china drip coffe pot, the stack set, the square leftover and the juicer. The bowl pictured below is a scarcely found ruffled, tab-handled serving piece which has also been found in a few decal patterns.

"Medallion"	Lettuce	Ivory	Other Colors
Bowl, #2	3.00-4.00	2.50-3.00	4.00-5.00
Bowl, #3	4.00-4.50	3.00-3.50	5.00-6.00
Bowl, #4	6.00-8.00	4.00-5.00	8.00-10.00
Bowl, #5	8.00-10.00	6.00-7.00	10.00-12.00
Bowl, #6	12.00-14.00	8.00-10.00	12.00-15.00
Bowl, 9¼" ruffled	30.00-35.00		
Casserole	15.00-18.00	9.00-11.00	18.00-20.00
Creamer	4.00-5.00	3.00-4.00	5.00-6.00
Custard	5.00-7.00	3.00-4.00	5.00-5.50
Drip coffee	55.00-65.00	25.00-30.00	65.00-70.00
Drip jar	9.00-11.00	7.00-9.00	10.00-12.00
Jug, ice lip, 4 pt.	9.00-11.00	7.00-9.00	10.00-12.00
Jug, ice lip, 5 pt.	14.00-16.00	8.00-10.00	13.00-15.00
Jug, 4¼", 5", 5½"	7.00-10.00	6.00-9.00	10.00-12.00
Jug, 6½", 7"	13.00-15.00	9.00-11.00	15.00-18.00
Leftover square	25.00-30.00	15.00-18.00	35.00-40.00
Reamer	250.00-300.00		375.00-425.00
Shakers, ea.	10.00-12.00	10.00-12.00	14.00-16.00
Stack set	45.00-50.00	22.00-27.00	40.00-50.00
Sugar and lid	7.00-9.00	6.00-8.00	8.00-10.00
Teapot	30.00-35.00	25.00-30.00	35.00-45.00

Ruffled tab-handled "Medallion" bowl.

Row 1: Leftover, square; custard; teapot. **Row 2:** Juicer; casserole; juicer. **Row 3:** Drip coffee; bowl #3; jug #5.

"Pert," Tab-Handled, Straight-Sided

The "Pert" kitchenware shape was introduced in 1941. It is most commonly found in the colors Chinese red/white and cadet/white. These pieces have solid colored bodies with contrasting Hi-white handles and knobs. Usually, the cadet/white colored items are found decorated with a floral decal such as Rose Parade. White bodied pieces in this shape also exist, and they are usually decorated with a decal of one of the kitchenware patterns.

A lid to the sugar has appeared. The limited number of lids which have surfaced indicate that a lid was not a regular feature for this style sugar. The rounded oval shape of this lid is significantly different from that of the two sizes of teapot lids. For a comparison of the three lids see the photo below.

The tab-handled and straight-sided shapes are frequently found in Chinese red or cadet with contrasting Hi-white features, and are associated with the "Pert" line. Tab-handled items normally found are a casserole, drip jar and bean pot. Straight-sided pieces which complement "Pert" kitchenware are a custard cup and four sizes of mixing bowls.

Kitchenware	Chinese Red	Cadet
Bean pot, tab-handled	30.00-35.00	25.00-27.00
Bowl, 5¼″ straight-sided	4.00-5.00	4.00-5.00
Bowl, 6″ straight-sided	6.00-7.00	5.00-6.00
Bowl, 7½″ straight-sided	7.00-9.00	7.00-9.00
Bowl, 9″ straight-sided	10.00-12.00	10.00-12.00
Casserole, tab-handled	18.00-20.00	16.00-18.00
Creamer, "Pert"	6.00-7.00	6.00-7.00
Custard, straight-sided	3.00-4.00	3.00-4.00
Drip jar, tab-handled	12.00-14.00	10.00-12.00
Jug, 5″ "Pert"	10.00-12.00	8.00-9.00
Jug, 6½″ "Pert"	14.00-16.00	9.00-11.00
Jug, 7½″ "Pert"	18.00-22.00	11.00-13.00
Shaker, "Pert," ea.	6.00-7.00	4.00-5.00
Sugar, "Pert"	6.00-7.00	6.00-7.00
Sugar lid, "Pert"	UND	UND
Teapot, 3-cup "Pert"	16.00-18.00	14.00-16.00
Teapot, 6-cup "Pert"	18.00-22.00	18.00-20.00

Left to right: "Pert" 3-cup teapot lid; "Pert" sugar lid; "Pert" 6-cup teapot lid.

Row 1: Jug, 7½″; jug, 6½″; jug, 5″. **Row 2:** Teapot, 6-cup; teapot, 3-cup; sugar; creamer. **Row 3:** Shakers; casserole, tab-handled; drip jar, tab-handled. **Row 4:** Bean pot, tab-handled; bowl, 7½″ straight-sided; bowl, 6″ straight-sided.

"Radiance"

Following the success of the first kitchenware line, Hall introduced a second shape–"Radiance"–in 1933. "Radiance" will be found in a variety of colors, but Chinese red is the most common and the most desirable to today's collectors. The easiest pieces to find are the mixing bowls and the medium-size jugs. However, the lids to most sizes of the jugs are not easily found. The hardest items to locate are the condiment jar and the all-china drip coffee pot. Although many cereal sets, which include four canisters and two matching shakers, have found their way into collectors hands, the demand for these sets has remained strong. The cereal set was introduced in 1938 and was produced in numerous colors. Many "Radiance" shape kitchenware items will be found used in the various decal lines.

A shape which is very similar to "Radiance" is the "Rayed" shape commonly associated with the Autumn Leaf pattern. "Rayed" shape pieces have a similar style and the same vertical lines in their body. The most significant difference is in the ear-shaped handles which are present on such items as the "Rayed" jugs, teapots and coffee pots.

"Radiance"	Red/Cobalt	Ivory	Other Colors
Bowl, #1, 3½″	3.50-4.50	2.00-3.00	3.00-4.00
Bowl, #2, 5¼″	4.00-5.00	2.50-3.00	4.00-5.00
Bowl, #3, 6″	5.00-6.00	3.00-3.50	4.00-5.00
Bowl, #4, 7½″	6.00-8.00	4.00-5.00	6.00-7.00
Bowl, #5, 9″	10.00-12.00	6.00-8.00	9.00-11.00
Bowl, #6, 10″	15.00-17.00	6.00-8.00	10.00-12.00
Canister, 2 qt.	60.00-65.00	18.00-20.00	50.00-55.00
Casserole	25.00-30.00	10.00-12.00	18.00-20.00
Condiment jar	UND	UND	UND
Drip coffee pot	95.00-110.00	25.00-30.00	65.00-70.00
Drip jar	15.00-17.00	7.00-9.00	12.00-14.00
Jug*, 3¼″ #1; 4¼″ #2	25.00-27.00	8.00-10.00	18.00-20.00
Jug*, 4¾″ #3; 5¼″ #4	30.00-32.00	10.00-12.00	20.00-22.00
Jug*, 6¼″ #5; 6¾″ #6	35.00-40.00	12.00-14.00	20.00-25.00
Shaker, canister style	14.00-16.00	8.00-10.00	12.00-15.00
Stack set	45.00-55.00	10.00-12.00	35.00-40.00
Teapot, 6-cup	60.00-70.00	20.00-25.00	45.00-55.00
*With lid			

Row 1: Cereal set canisters. **Row 2:** Cereal set shakers; bowl, 6″; teapot. **Row 3:** Jug and cover, 6¼″; jug and cover, 5¼″; jug and cover, 4¼″.

"Sundial"

The "Sundial" kitchenware shape was introduced in 1938. The most commonly found color is Chinese red. The casseroles, sugars and creamers, individual teapots and coffee pots will be found in a number of sizes and some of these pieces are still being made.

The hardest pieces to find are the coffee server and the cookie jar. The wholesale price of the cookie jar in 1940 was $2.00. Today, a cookie jar in cobalt or red will bring over $100.00.

"Sundial"	Red/Cobalt	Other Colors
Batter jug	40.00-45.00	35.00-40.00
Casserole, #1, 4¾"	10.00-12.00	7.00-9.00
Casserole, #2, 5¼"	10.00-12.00	8.00-10.00
Casserole, #3, 6½"	12.00-14.00	8.00-10.00
Casserole, #4, 8"	18.00-22.00	12.00-15.00
Creamer	5.00-7.00	3.00-5.00
Coffee pot, individual	27.00-32.00	18.00-20.00
Coffee server	125.00-150.00	UND
Cookie jar	95.00-110.00	UND
Sugar	5.00-7.00	3.00-5.00
Syrup	35.00-40.00	25.00-30.00
*Teapot, individual	30.00-35.00	8.00-12.00
Teapot, six-cup	55.00-65.00	35.00-45.00

*Currently being produced in numerous colors.

Row 1: Cookie jar; coffee server; teapot, six-cup. **Row 2:** Batter jug; coffee pot, individual; sugar and creamer. **Row 3:** Syrup; casserole, 5¼″; casserole, 8″.

Kitchenware Patterns
Acacia and Beauty

Acacia is a 1940's pattern which is not easy to find. Most of the pieces which have been turning up are in the "Radiance" shape. The appearance of the all-china drip coffee pot, and the "Radiance" teapot, stack set and covered jugs has generated renewed interest in this pattern among collectors. Dinnerware with this decal has been found. However, all the dinnerware found to date has been made by Taylor, Smith and Taylor. Hall purists may not find a mixture acceptable, but the two styles of pottery look nice together.

The name "Beauty" will usually have a color associated with it as collectors attempt to distinguish the color background upon which the decal has been placed.

For example, if the decal is used on an item with a totally white background, then the piece is referred to as "White Beauty." Pieces of "Black Beauty" will have parts with a Hi-black glaze. However, the colorful orange and black decal will appear on a portion which has a Hi-white glaze. Very few kitchenware pieces with this decal are being found and no dinnerware is known. Among the items most frequently seen are the "Radiance" casserole, and the handled shakers with a white background. The casserole shown on the bottom left in the metal holder has the Forman Brothers backstamp. The 12" round bowl on the right side of the bottom shelf is unusual. It has a light yellow glaze and is trimmed in platinum.

Kitchenware	Acacia	Beauty
Bean pot, New England #4	75.00-80.00	65.00-75.00
Bowl, 9½" salad		12.00-14.00
Bowl, 12" salad		25.00-35.00
Bowl, 6" "Radiance"	6.00-9.00	
Bowl, 7½" "Radiance"	10.00-12.00	
Bowl, 9" "Radiance"	12.00-14.00	
Casserole, (Forman) 2-handled		25.00-30.00
Casserole, "Medallion"	32.00-35.00	
Casserole, "Radiance"	30.00-32.00	32.00-35.00
Casserole, "Thick Rim"		32.00-35.00
Drip coffee pot, all-china "Radiance"	85.00-95.00	

Kitchenware	Acacia	Beauty
Custard	4.00-5.00	
Drip jar and lid, "Radiance"	12.00-15.00	
Jug*, "Radiance" #2	40.00-45.00	
Jug*, "Radiance" #3, #4	45.00-55.00	
Jug*, "Radiance" #5, #6	50.00-55.00	
Marmite and cover	25.00-27.00	27.00-30.00
Shakers, handled ea.	7.50-9.00	
Stack set, "Radiance"	45.00-55.00	55.00-65.00
Teapot, "Radiance"	85.00-95.00	
Teapot, "Rutherford"		75.00-90.00

*With cover

Acacia teapot, "Radiance" shape.

Row 1: Acacia jug, "Radiance"; Acacia bowl, 7½" "Radiance"; Acacia shakers, handled. **Row 2:** Ivory Beauty bean pot, New England #4; Ivory Beauty shakers, handled. **Row 3:** Ivory Beauty casserole, 2-handled Forman Brothers; Lemon Beauty 12" salad bowl.

Blue Blossom

Blue Blossom is a blue-body decal kitchenware line which was introduced in 1939. The decal consists of an elongated green leaf tipped with a colorful red, yellow and white iris-like flower. A Blue Blossom morning tea set has been found advertised in a 1940's Blackwell-Wieland Company wholesale catalog. It is referred to in that catalog as an "Apple Blossom" pattern. The wholesale price for the entire set–teapot, sugar, creamer and lids–was $2.60. Notice the teapot and creamer are the same shape as the No. 1 Tea Set teapot and creamer. However, the sugar to the Blue Blossom set has handles and a lid. The sugar to the No. 1 Tea Set is handleless and has no lid. Also, no cups, saucers or plates have been found with the Blue Blossom set.

It seems as if new shapes with this decal are being uncovered almost daily. Significant new discoveries include canisters and matching shakers, an Airflow teapot and a "Zephyr" style butter and leftover. Other interesting pieces new to the listing are a New York sugar and creamer, "Five Band" jugs in two sizes, a "Thick Rim" drip jar and several different shapes of casseroles.

Considering the relatively high price of the more desirable pieces of this pattern, collector interest is almost unbelievable. New collectors are aggressively competing with seasoned veterans for the limited supply and the prices are gradually rising.

Row 1: Ball jug #4; Ball jug #3; Ball jug #2; Ball jug #1. **Row 2:** Teapot, "Sundial"; Teapot, Streamline; cookie jar, "Five Band." **Row 3:** Butter, 1# "Zephyr"; leftover, "Zephyr"; syrup, "Sundial." **Row 4:** Batter jug, "Sundial"; bean pot, New England #4; leftover, loop-handled.

Kitchenware	Price	Kitchenware	Price
Ball jug #1	45.00-55.00	Creamer, morning	25.00-32.00
Ball jug #2	47.00-55.00	Creamer, New York	20.00-25.00
Ball jug #3	40.00-50.00	Custard, "Thick Rim"	12.00-14.00
Ball jug #4	55.00-60.00	Drip jar, #1188 open	25.00-30.00
Batter jug, "Sundial"	95.00-110.00	Drip jar and cover, "Thick Rim"	35.00-40.00
Bean pot, New England #4	110.00-125.00	Jug, 1½ pt. "Five Band"	30.00-40.00
Bowl, 6" "Thick Rim"	27.00-30.00	Jug, 2 qt. "Five Band"	40.00-45.00
Bowl, 7½" "Thick Rim"	25.00-30.00	Jug, loop handle	50.00-55.00
Bowl, 8½" "Thick Rim"	27.00-35.00	Leftover, loop handle	60.00-65.00
Butter, 1# "Zephyr"-style	UND	Leftover, "Zephyr"-style	80.00-90.00
Canister, "Radiance"	95.00-110.00	Shakers, "Five Band," ea.	12.50-15.00
Casserole, #76 round, handled	27.00-35.00	Shakers, handled, ea. (4)	14.00-16.00
Casserole, #77 round, handled	30.00-35.00	Shakers, "Radiance" canister-style, ea.	30.00-35.00
Casserole, #100 oval	30.00-40.00	Shirred egg dish	45.00-50.00
Casserole, "Five Band"	35.00-45.00	Sugar and lid, morning	30.00-37.00
Casserole, "Sundial" #1	35.00-40.00	Sugar and lid, New York	25.00-30.00
Casserole, "Sundial" #4	37.00-45.00	Syrup, "Sundial"	85.00-95.00
Casserole, "Thick Rim"	35.00-42.00	Teapot, Airflow	110.00-130.00
Coffee server, "Sundial"	190.00-250.00	Teapot, morning	95.00-120.00
Cookie jar, "Five Band"	80.00-95.00	Teapot, "Sundial"	95.00-110.00
Cookie jar, "Sundial"	150.00-200.00	Teapot, Streamline	110.00-130.00

Row 1: Jug, loop-handled; cookie jar, "Sundial"; shakers, handled. **Row 2:** Teapot, morning set; sugar and creamer, morning set; shakers, "Five Band." **Row 3:** Casserole, "Thick Rim"; casserole, individual "Sundial"; shirred egg dish; custard, "Thick Rim."

Blue Garden

Blue Garden is a decal kitchenware pattern employing a floral decal on a cobalt body. The delicate white flowers and green leaves are not as colorful as the decoration on the Blue Blossom pattern, but they are still attractive enough to perk collector interest.

The discovery of an amazing number of previously unlisted pieces in this pattern has also sparked collector interest. Prizes such as the "Sundial" coffee server, "Zephyr" style water bottle, butter or leftover are bound to attract a lot of attention in any collection. Some veteran Hall collectors, who had previously thought Blue Garden contained an insignificant number of pieces, are now looking at this pattern again. Both old and new collectors are finding the search for these pieces is not effortless. The only item anyone is finding in abundance is the "Sundial" #4 casserole. Most other pieces are scarce, but the list of known items continues to grow and so does the number of collectors.

Left to right: Ball jug #3; coffee server, "Sundial"; jug, loop-handled.

Kitchenware	Price
Ball jug	40.00-45.00
Batter jug, "Sundial"	90.00-110.00
Bean pot, New England #4	85.00-95.00
Bowl, 6" "Thick Rim"	18.00-20.00
Bowl, 7½" "Thick Rim"	20.00-22.00
Bowl, 8½" "Thick Rim"	25.00-27.00
Butter, 1# "Zephyr"-style	150.00-200.00
Canister, "Radiance"	90.00-100.00
Casserole, "Sundial" #1	25.00-30.00
Casserole, "Sundial" #4	20.00-25.00
Coffee server, "Sundial"	160.00-190.00
Cookie jar, "Five Band"	65.00-70.00
Cookie jar, "Sundial"	120.00-140.00
Creamer, morning	20.00-25.00
Creamer, New York	18.00-22.00
Custard, "Thick Rim"	8.00-10.00
Drip jar, #1188 open	22.00-27.00
Drip jar and cover, "Thick Rim"	25.00-30.00
Jug, loop handle	40.00-45.00

Kitchenware	Price
Leftover, loop handle	45.00-55.00
Leftover, "Zephyr"-style	75.00-85.00
Shakers, handled, ea. (4)	12.00-14.00
Sugar and lid, morning	25.00-30.00
Sugar and lid, New York	22.00-25.00
Syrup, "Sundial"	80.00-90.00
Teapot, Airflow	110.00-120.00
Teapot, Aladdin	95.00-110.00
Teapot, morning	90.00-110.00
Teapot, New York	85.00-95.00
Teapot, "Sundial"	110.00-120.00
Teapot, Streamline	110.00-130.00
Water bottle, "Zephyr"-style	95.00-110.00

Row 1: Teapot, "Sundial"; teapot, Streamline; water bottle, "Zephyr." **Row 2:** Batter jug, "Sundial"; jug, 1½ pt. "Five Band"; butter, "Zephyr." **Row 3:** Shaker, handled; sugar and creamer, morning set shape; leftover, loop-handled. **Row 4:** Casserole, "Sundial"; Bowl, 6″ "Thick Rim".

"Blue Floral"

The "Blue Floral" pattern consists of a set of three mixing bowls and a casserole. The bowls have cadet blue exteriors and white interiors with a tiny floral sprig decoration. The casserole has a cadet blue base and a white lid with a large blue knob. The floral decoration on the casserole is on the white part of the lid. This pattern was made for the Jewel Tea Company during the mid-1940's. The casserole retailed for $2.00 and the three piece bowl set was $3.50.

"Blue Floral"	Price
Bowl, 6¼"	4.00-5.00
Bowl, 7¾"	5.00-6.00
Bowl, 9"	7.00-9.00
Casserole	10.00-12.00

Blue Willow

The Blue Willow decal is only being found on a few pieces, and the reports of collectors finding these pieces are infrequent. Perhaps the most exciting news to teapot collectors is the existence of this decoration on three different size Boston teapots.

The casserole will be found in two sizes. The bottom is pictured in the photo. The lid features the Blue Willow pattern, is gently domed and has a knob handle. Although most of Hall's Blue Willow which collectors have been finding appears to date to the early 1920's, the ashtray has been made recently. It has the new backstamp which would place it in the post 1970 era. Also, the decal lacks the quality and fine detail of the decals on the earlier pieces.

Row 1: Teapot, 2-cup Boston; teapot, 4-cup Boston; Chinese teacup. **Row 2:** Shallow finger bowl; casserole bottom; ashtray.

Blue Willow Kitchenware	Price
Ashtray	6.00-7.00
Bowl, finger	12.00-15.00
Bowl, Plum Pudding	12.00-15.00
Casserole, 5"	25.00-30.00
Casserole, 7½"	30.00-35.00
Teacup, Chinese (2 styles)	12.00-15.00
Teapot, 2-cup Boston	60.00-65.00
Teapot, 4-cup Boston	60.00-70.00
Teapot, 6-cup Boston	70.00-75.00

Cactus

According to an article in the trade magazine *China, Glass and Lamps*, Hall introduced the Cactus pattern to retailers at trade shows in January, 1937. The article described the pattern as "blending shades of green, yellow, red, orange, blue, brown and gray." The decal appeared on a new Hall kitchenware shape which was also being introduced in various solid colors. The new shape was not named in the article but the illustration pictures the shape we are calling "Five Band." Items with the Cactus decal originally introduced on the "Five Band" shape were as follows: cookie jar, covered syrup, shakers, two sizes of jugs, three sizes of mixing bowls, a casserole and a batter bowl.

Hall also used the Cactus decal on other shapes. One of the most commonly found items is the "Viking" Drip-O-lator coffee pot which was made for the Enterprise Aluminum Company of Massilon, Ohio. Enterprise supplied the aluminum dripper and marketed the finished product under its Drip-O-lator trademark. A covered sugar and creamer in this shape may also be found with diligent searching.

Notice the different decals on the two pair of "Five Band" shakers in the photograph. Hall often used pieces of a decal to decorate smaller items. In some patterns these partial decals may present an identification problem. However, since the Cactus decal is small and easily identified, items with partial decals in this pattern are quickly categorized.

Kitchenware	Price
Ball jug #3	30.00-32.00
Batter bowl, "Five Band"	27.00-30.00
Bowl, 6″ "Five Band"	10.00-12.00
Bowl, 7¼″ "Five Band"	12.00-15.00
Bowl, 8¾″ "Five Band"	15.00-18.00
Bowl, 6″ "Radiance"	10.00-12.00
Bowl, 7½″ "Radiance"	12.00-15.00
Bowl, 9″ "Radiance"	15.00-18.00
Casserole, "Five Band"	30.00-35.00
Casserole, "Radiance"	30.00-35.00
Coffee pot, "Five Band"	25.00-27.00
Coffee pot, "Viking" Drip-O-lator	25.00-27.00
Cookie jar, "Five Band"	45.00-55.00
Creamer, New York	10.00-12.00
Creamer, "Viking"	10.00-12.00
Jug, 1½″ pt. "Five Band"	35.00-45.00
Jug, 2 qt. "Five Band"	40.00-45.00
Onion soup, individual	35.00-45.00
Shakers, "Five Band," ea.	12.00-15.00
Shakers, handled, ea.	12.00-15.00
Stack set, "Radiance"	50.00-55.00
Sugar and lid, New York	12.00-15.00
Sugar and lid, "Viking"	12.00-15.00
Syrup, "Five Band"	32.00-37.00
Teapot, French	45.00-55.00

Row 1: Cookie jar, "Five Band"; jug, 2 qt. "Five Band"; jug, 1½ pt. "Five Band." **Row 2:** Ball jug #3; teapot, French; shakers, "Five Band." **Row 3:** Individual onion soup, sugar and creamer, New York; shakers, "Five Band." **Row 4:** Bowl, 9″ "Radiance"; batter bowl, "Five Band"; syrup, "Five Band."

Carrot and Golden Carrot

Although it is possible to assemble a collection of Hall's Carrot pattern, much diligent searching will be required to find many of the pieces. The Carrot/Golden Carrot kitchenware listing has turned out to be more extensive than many collectors originally anticipated. However, the number of items with gold decoration is still quite limited. Only the Windshield teapot, the Zeisel cookie jar, the #68 casserole, the 12½″ Welsh rarebit and the three-piece "Thick Rim" bowl set have been reported with gold trim. Of these pieces, the teapot is found most frequently, but it is also the most desirable item, which keeps the price relatively high.

Kitchenware	Price
Ball jug #3	30.00-32.00
Batter bowl, "Five Band"	30.00-35.00
Bean pot, New England #4	55.00-65.00
Bowl, 6″ "Five Band"	10.00-12.00
Bowl, 7¼″ "Five Band"	12.00-15.00
Bowl, 8¾″ "Five Band"	15.00-18.00
Bowl, 6″ "Radiance"	10.00-12.00
Bowl, 7½″ "Radiance"	12.00-15.00
Bowl, 9″ "Radiance"	15.00-18.00
Bowl, 10″ "Radiance"	18.00-22.00
Bowl, 6″ "Thick Rim"	10.00-12.00
Bowl, 7½″ "Thick Rim"	12.00-15.00

Kitchenware	Price
Bowl, 8½″ "Thick Rim"	15.00-18.00
Casserole, #65, #68, #70	25.00-30.00
Casserole, "Radiance"	25.00-30.00
Cookie jar, "Five Band"	55.00-60.00
Cookie jar, Zeisel	60.00-65.00
Dish, 12½″ Welsh rarebit	25.00-30.00
Jug, #5 "Radiance"	25.00-30.00
Shaker, "Five Band," ea.	12.00-14.00
Shaker, "Novelty Radiance," ea.	15.00-18.00
Stack set, "Radiance"	50.00-55.00
Syrup, "Five Band"	50.00-55.00
Teapot, Windshield	45.00-55.00

Row 1: Ball jug #3; casserole, "Radiance"; bean pot, New England #4. **Row 2:** Dish, 12½″ Wesh rarebit; shakers, "Novelty Radiance."

Clover and Golden Clover

The clover decal is a very stylized and colorful red, blue and green decal. Items with this decal will be found both with and without gold decoration. Pieces which are gold encrusted are called "Golden Clover." According to Hall ads, the Golden Clover line consists of the Windshield teapot, the #68 round casserole, the "big-earred" Zeisel cookie jar and the three-piece "Thick Rim" mixing bowl set. However, as may be seen from the photo, other pieces with gold decoration may be found.

Row 1: Teapot, Windshield; cookie jar, Zeisel-style. **Row 2:** Jug, 1½ pt. "Five Band"; shakers, handled.

Kitchenware	Price
Ball jug #3	30.00-35.00
Batter bowl, "Five Band"	30.00-35.00
Bowl, 6″ "Radiance"	10.00-12.00
Bowl, 7½″ "Radiance"	12.00-14.00
Bowl, 9″ "Radiance"	14.00-16.00
Bowl, 6″ "Thick Rim"	10.00-12.00
Bowl, 7½″ "Thick Rim"	12.00-14.00
Bowl, 8½″ "Thick Rim"	14.00-16.00
Casserole, #65, #68, #70	25.00-30.00
Casserole, "Radiance"	25.00-30.00
Cookie jar, Zeisel-style	55.00-65.00
Jug, #5 "Radiance"	18.00-22.00
Shaker, handled, ea. (4)	12.00-15.00
Teapot, Windshield	45.00-55.00

Eggshell Buffet Service

Hall's Eggshell Buffet service with the Dot design is a line with a large number of pieces. The most frequently found color of Dot is red, but other colored dots such as green, blue and orange will also be seen. Generally, the dots are found on an eggshell body, but some pieces with an ivory body are also available. An example of the ivory body with red dots is the pair of handled shakers on the bottom row. Also shown on the bottom row is a pretzel jar with a "half dot" decal. Half of the dot is completed by the bottom and the other half is formed by lining the lid up correctly. A "Radiance" casserole with an ivory body and the "half dot" decal also exists.

As may be seen from the listing, the Dot design appears on some kitchenware shapes which are not usually found in other decorated patterns. Examples of these are the handled cocotte, the #691 Drip coffee and the buffet-style round and oval casseroles. The "Thin Rim" bowls and the custard may be found either smooth or with vertical ribs. The 13½″ fish-shaped salad is part of the set even though it only has matching trim and does not have any dots. This platter is still being made in numerous colors and now comes in two different sizes.

The pieces appearing most often are the handled shakers. Many teapot collectors are still eagerly waiting to acquire the "Rutherford" teapot. Another hard-to-find piece is the Tom and Jerry bowl.

In addition to the Dot pattern illustrated here, some pieces of the Buffet Service will be found in other patterns. One example is the "Swag" pattern as seen on the shakers in the photo. Another pattern which we have not yet seen is a hand painted "Plaid" design.

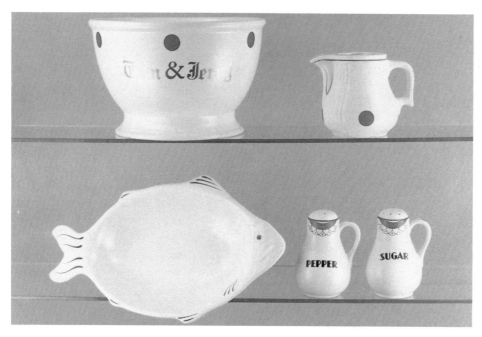

Row 1: Tom & Jerry bowl, Jug and cover, "Radiance" #3. **Row 2:** Fish-shape baker; shakers, handled (Swag pattern).

Kitchenware	Red Dot	Other Colors	Kitchenware	Red Dot	Other Colors
Bean pot, New England #3	40.00-45.00	35.00-40.00	Drip, #1188 open	15.00-18.00	12.00-15.00
Bean pot, New England #4	45.00-50.00	40.00-45.00	Drip coffee, #691	80.00-90.00	70.00-80.00
Bowl, 8¾″ salad	10.00-12.00	8.00-10.00	Fish-shape salad, 13½″	30.00-35.00	
Bowl, 9¾″ salad	10.00-12.00	8.00-10.00	Host jug	50.00-60.00	
Bowl, 8½″ "Thin Rim"	10.00-12.00	10.00-12.00	Jug and cover, "Radiance" #3	25.00-30.00	22.00-25.00
Bowl, 7¼″ "Thin Rim"	7.00-9.00	7.00-9.00	Jug and cover, "Radiance" #5	27.00-32.00	25.00-27.00
Bowl, 6¼″ "Thin Rim"	6.00-8.00	6.00-8.00	Mug, Tom & Jerry	6.00-9.00	6.00-9.00
Bowl, ftd. Tom & Jerry	75.00-85.00	70.00-80.00	Mustard	20.00-25.00	
Casserole, 9¾″ oval	22.00-27.00	22.00-27.00	Pretzel jar	45.00-55.00	45.00-55.00
Casserole, 8½″, 9¼″ round	22.00-27.00	22.00-27.00	Shakers, handled, ea. (4)	7.00-9.00	7.00-9.00
Cocotte, 4″ handled	12.00-14.00	10.00-12.00	Shirred egg dish	18.00-22.00	16.00-18.00
Custard, "Ribbed"	3.00-4.00	3.00-4.00	Teapot, "Rutherford"	55.00-65.00	55.00-65.00

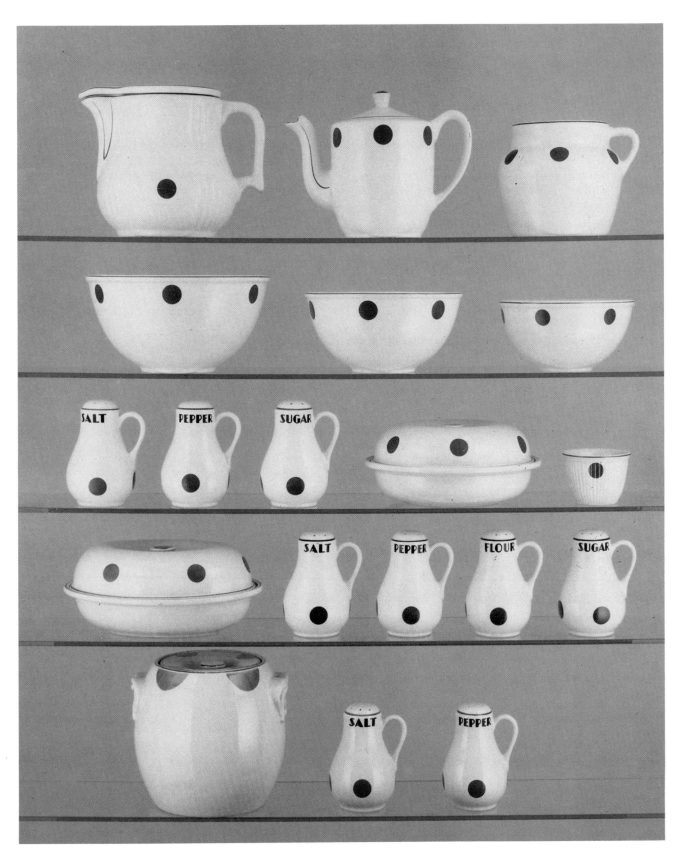

Row 1: Jug, "Radiance" #5; teapot, "Rutherford"; bean pot, New England #3. **Row 2:** Bowl, "Thin Rim" 8½"; bowl, "Thin Rim" 7¼"; bowl, "Thin Rim" 6¼". **Row 3:** Shakers, handled; casserole, round; custard, "Ribbed." **Row 4:** Casserole, oval; shakers, handled. **Row 5:** Pretzel jar, "Half Dot" on ivory body; shakers, handled, Red Dot on ivory body.

Fantasy

Fantasy is a very colorful–almost gaudy–floral decal which is found infrequently. Most pieces are also neatly trimmed with a narrow red band. The only commonly found pieces are the handled shakers and all styles of casseroles. Special finds would include the coffee server, loop handle leftover and the morning tea set. Finding a Streamline teapot in Fantasy would send most any teapot collector to dreamland.

Kitchenware	Price
Ball jug #1	40.00-50.00
Ball jug #2	40.00-50.00
Ball jug #3	40.00-50.00
Ball jug #4	45.00-55.00
Batter jug, "Sundial"	110.00-125.00
Bean pot, New England #4	60.00-70.00
Bowl, 6″ "Thick Rim"	10.00-12.00
Bowl, 7½″ "Thick Rim"	12.00-15.00
Bowl, 8½″ "Thick Rim"	15.00-18.00
Casserole, "Radiance"	30.00-35.00
Casserole, "Thick Rim"	30.00-35.00
Casserole, "Sundial"	30.00-35.00
Coffee server, "Sundial"	190.00-225.00

Kitchenware	Price
Creamer, morning	15.00-18.00
Creamer, New York	15.00-18.00
Custard, "Thick Rim"	9.00-12.00
Drip jar, #1188 open	22.00-27.00
Drip jar and cover, "Thick Rim"	22.00-27.00
Jug, Donut	75.00-85.00
Leftover, loop handled	32.00-37.00
Shakers, handled, ea.	15.00-18.00
Sugar and lid, morning	18.00-22.00
Syrup, "Sundial"	95.00-110.00
Teapot, morning	85.00-95.00
Teapot, Streamline	150.00-175.00

Teapot, Streamline.

Row 1: Batter jug, "Sundial"; casserole, "Thick Rim." **Row 2:** Shakers, handled; Ball jug #1; sugar and creamer, morning set shape.

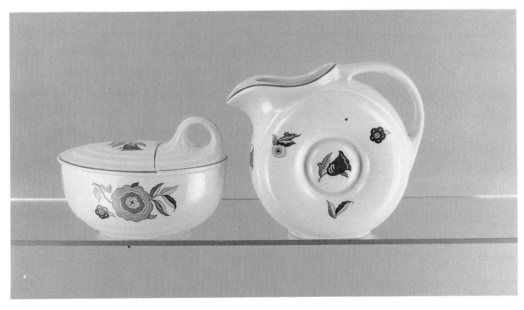

Leftover, loop handled; jug, Donut.

Flamingo and Floral Lattice

The Flamingo listing as a kitchenware pattern is new to this book. Previously, the decal had been listed as appearing on the "Viking" Drip-O-lator which Hall made for the Enterprise Aluminum Company. Other pieces with this decal have now been found. A "Viking" covered sugar and creamer may be seen in the photograph. Collectors will find this decal more commonly on the "Five Band" batter bowl and the "Viking" Drip-O-lator coffee pot. Other interesting pieces are the #691 drip coffee pot, the Streamline teapot, and the "Five Band" cookie jar. These are pieces which are extremely desirable, but very hard to find. Any Streamline teapots appearing on the market are eagerly snatched by teapot collectors.

Floral Lattice kitchenware has a decal which consists of a vine-like potted flower that is intertwined in a lattice framework. This mini-floral decal may be frequently spotted on the "Five Band" batter bowl and syrup. Other pieces in this pattern are not easily found. Notice some pieces are trimmed in red while others are trimmed with platinum bands.

Kitchenware	Flamingo	Floral Lattice
Ball jug #3		25.00-30.00
Batter bowl, "Five Band"	35.00-40.00	18.00-20.00
Bowl, 6″ "Five Band"		8.00-10.00
Bowl, 7½″ "Five Band"		10.00-12.00
Bowl, 8¾″ "Five Band"		12.00-14.00
Canister, "Radiance"		65.00-75.00
Casserole, "Five Band"	35.00-40.00	
Casserole, #99 oval		25.00-30.00
Casserole, #76 round		25.00-30.00
Casserole, #101 round		25.00-30.00
Coffee pot, "Viking" Drip-O-lator	25.00-27.00	25.00-30.00
Cookie jar, "Five Band"	65.00-75.00	55.00-65.00
Creamer, "Viking"	14.00-18.00	
Drip coffee pot, #691	85.00-95.00	
Onion soup, individual		22.00-27.00
Shakers, canister style, ea.		18.00-20.00
Shakers, handled, ea.	12.00-14.00	10.00-12.00
Sugar and lid, "Viking"	18.00-22.00	
Syrup, "Five Band"	35.00-45.00	18.00-22.00
Teapot, Streamline	95.00-110.00	

Left to right: Flamingo "Five Band" cookie jar; Floral Lattice #99 oval casserole.

Row 1: Flamingo Drip coffee pot, #691; Flamingo coffee pot, "Viking" Drip-O-later; Flamingo syrup, "Five Band." **Row 2:** Flamingo batter bowl, "Five Band"; Flamingo creamer and sugar, "Five Band." **Row 3:** Floral Lattice canister, "Radiance"; Floral Lattice batter bowl, "Five Band"; Floral Lattice individual onion soup; Floral Lattice syrup, "Five Band."

Flareware

Flareware is essentially a serving-type kitchenware line which was offered by Hall in the early 1960's. Basic decorations were Autumn Leaf, Gold Lace, Chestnut and Radial. Today the only decoration found in any quantity is Gold Lace. A common variation of the Gold Lace decoration includes pieces found with the Heather Rose decal used in combination with the star-like gold Lace design. The Flareware Autumn Leaf has nothing in common with the Autumn Leaf dinnerware pattern shown earlier in this book which was distributed by Jewel Tea. An example of the pattern may be seen on the cookie jar in the center of the picture. The Radial design has thin black vertical lines over a white base. Pieces of the Chestnut pattern have an all-over brown glaze.

The coffee server was designed to be used with the brass and wooden three-legged candle warmer. Another multi-purpose three-legged warmer, made of china, was used with the teapot, coffee urn and casserole. The coffee urn is shaped like the cookie jar and has a spigot to dispense coffee instead of a pour spout. The brass warmer has no design and was used with all the patterns. Therefore, it will only be listed once in the price guide below.

Kitchenware	Gold Lace	Autumn Leaf	Heather Rose	Radial
Bowl, 6″	3.00-4.00	3.00-4.00	4.00-5.00	2.00-3.00
Bowl, 7″	4.00-6.00	4.00-5.00	6.00-8.00	3.00-4.00
Bowl, 8″	6.00-8.00	5.00-7.00	8.00-10.00	4.00-5.00
Bowl, salad	7.00-9.00	6.00-7.00	9.00-11.00	4.00-5.00
Casserole, 3 pt.	10.00-12.00	6.00-8.00		5.00-7.00
Casserole, 2 qt.	12.00-15.00	10.00-12.00	14.00-16.00	9.00-11.00
Coffee server, 15-cup	20.00-25.00	12.00-14.00		12.00-14.00
Coffee urn, 15-cup	35.00-40.00	18.00-22.00	18.00-22.00	12.00-15.00
Cookie jar	12.00-15.00	12.00-15.00		10.00-12.00
Teapot, 6-cup	30.00-35.00	18.00-22.00		15.00-18.00
Trivet, china	10.00-12.00			
Warmer, brass	5.00-6.00			

Row 1: Cookie jar with Heather Rose decal; cookie jar with Autumn Leaf decal; teapot with Gold Lace design. **Row 2:** Casserole, 2 qt. with Gold Lace design; bowl with Heather Rose decal; coffee server, Gold Lace design with brass and wooden candle warmer.

Golden Glo

Golden Glo is a Hall kitchenware line which dates back to the 1940's and is still in production today. As a result of this long period of production, many different pieces have been subjected to this gold treatment. The gold color top glaze is normally applied over a Hi-white base. An example of the gold color backstamp used on older Golden Glo pieces is shown below. Pieces made after 1970 will have the new square backstamp. According to information contained in its backstamp, the oval casserole with the basketweave pattern was made for Bump's of San Francisco.

Row 1: Coffee pot, Coffee set shape; jug, "Five Band"; bean pot, New England #4. **Row 2:** Casserole, oval with basketweave pattern; casserole, #100, 8½" oval.

Golden Glo Kitchenware	Price
Ashtray, shell-shape	2.00-3.00
Baking shell, 4"	2.00-3.00
Baker, French, 7¼"	5.00-6.00
Baker, French, 8½"	6.00-8.00
Bean pot, New England #4	18.00-20.00
Bowl, Medallion, #3, #4, #5	7.00-10.00
Bowl, salad 9¾"	6.00-8.00
Casserole, duck knob	12.00-15.00
Casserole, french side handle, 4¼", 8¼", 10¼"	8.00-15.00
Casserole, oval, #100, #101, #103	10.00-12.00
Casserole, round, #75, #76, #78	10.00-12.00
Coffee pot, coffee set shape	18.00-20.00
Creamer, Boston	4.00-5.00
Creamer, coffee set shape	4.00-5.00
Creamer, morning set shape	4.00-5.00
Jug, "Five Band"	7.00-9.00

Golden Glo Kitchenware	Price
Mug, Irish coffee	7.00-9.00
Shakers, handled, ea.	7.00-8.00
Sugar, Boston	6.00-8.00
Sugar, coffee set shape	4.00-5.00
Sugar, morning set shape	6.00-8.00
Teapot, Aladdin	30.00-35.00
Teapot, Boston	18.00-22.00
Teapot, morning set shape	20.00-25.00

GOLDEN GLO
(HALL)
MADE IN U.S.A.
WARRANTED
22 CARAT GOLD
783

Golden Glo backstamp.

Gold Label Kitchenware

Hall selected 12 teapot shapes from the Gold Decorated line in the mid-1950's and added additional gold decoration to produce the Gold Label line. Each shape teapot in this new line exhibits a singular new gold decoration and may be identified through a gold code number on the bottom followed by the letters "GL." The handles, spouts and knobs of the lids to these teapots are covered with gold.

In addition to the teapots, eight kitchenware shapes were also selected for use in the Gold Label line. Includ-ed were the 9″ salad bowl, "Terrace" coffee pot, Zeisel cookie jar, "Rayed" jug, the #101 round casserole and the three-piece "Thick Rim" bowl set. As may be seen in the photograph, a French baker also exists in the squiggle design, but we have not seen this piece in the other gold designs.

The following listing provides the names of the teapots and the name associated with the design as assigned by researchers.

Teapot	Design	Price
Aladdin	Swag	30.00-37.00
Albany	Reflection	40.00-45.00
Baltimore	Nova	30.00-35.00
Boston	Fleur-de-lis	30.00-35.00
French	Daisy	25.00-30.00
Hollywood	Grid	25.00-30.00
Hook Cover	Star	18.00-20.00
Los Angeles	Medallion	25.00-30.00
New York	Flower	22.00-27.00
Parade	Squiggle	18.00-20.00
Philadelphia	Basket	20.00-25.00
Windshield	Dot	18.00-22.00

Kitchenware Accessories	Price
Bowl, 6″ "Thick Rim"	6.00-8.00
Bowl, 7½″ "Thick Rim"	8.00-10.00
Bowl, 9″ "Thick Rim"	12.00-14.00
Bowl, 9″ salad	10.00-12.00
Casserole, #101 round	20.00-27.00
Coffee pot, "Terrace"	22.00-27.00
Cookie jar, Zeisel	18.00-22.00
Jug, "Rayed"	9.00-11.00

HALL TEAPOTS 744

GROUP 901 GOLD LABEL

1411 ALADDIN (MARINE)

1412 WINDSHIELD (CAMELLIA)

124 BALTIMORE (MAROON)

1420 HOOK COVER (JADE)

204 PHILADELPHIA (TURQUOISE)

1432 PARADE (CANARY)

Six cup size, six shapes, Gold decorations on Ivory.

(233 706) 001 Asst (6)   Each Asst th $4.95

Shipper 1 Asst. - 20 lbs.

Row 1: Cookie jar, Zeisel, medallion design; teapot, Windshield, dot design; cookie jar, Zeisel, dot design. **Row 2:** Teapot, New York, flower design; teapot, Hook Cover, star design; teapot, Aladdin, swag design. **Row 3:** Casserole, #101 round, basket design; cookie jar, Zeisel, squiggle design; jug, "Rayed," squiggle design. **Row 4:** Casserole, #101 round, squiggle design; bowl, 9″ salad, squiggle design; baker, French, squiggle design.

Meadow Flower

Hall's use of the Meadow Flower decal dates to the late 1930's. Many collectors find these red-trimmed pieces with their colorful variegated floral decals quite attractive. Although the list of known shapes with this decal is gradually increasing, none of the pieces is easy to find.

The most significant discoveries have been a canister set and the Streamline teapot. The existence of the canisters means the canister-style shakers should exist, but to date no one has reported finding them.

Kitchenware	Price
Ball jug, #3	40.00-45.00
Bean pot, New England #4	75.00-85.00
Bowl, 6″ "Thick Rim"	10.00-12.00
Bowl, 7½″ "Thick Rim"	15.00-18.00
Bowl, 8½″ "Thick Rim"	18.00-22.00
Canister, "Radiance"	95.00-110.00
Casserole, "Radiance"	25.00-28.00

Kitchenware	Price
Casserole, "Thick Rim"	25.00-30.00
Cookie jar, "Five Band"	85.00-95.00
Custard, "Thick Rim"	8.00-10.00
Drip jar, #1188 open	22.00-27.00
Drip jar and cover, "Thick Rim"	18.00-22.00
Shakers, handled, ea.	14.00-16.00
Teapot, Streamline	175.00-225.00

Row 1: Bowl, 8½″ "Thick Rim"; bowl, 6″ "Thick Rim"; shakers, handled. **Row 2:** Canister, "Radiance" flour; canister, "Radiance" tea; Ball jug #3; custard, "Thick Rim."

Morning Glory

The Morning Glory kitchenware line was produced by Hall during the 1940's to coordinate with the Wildwood dinnerware pattern of the Jewel Company. Morning Glory, like Autumn Leaf, was a decal which was reserved exclusively for use on pieces produced for the Jewel Tea Company of Barrington, Illinois. The pieces have a cadet body with contrasting Hi-white areas which contain the morning glory decal.

The most significant discovery since the last book has been the appearance of an all-china drip coffee maker. While these are not common, several have been found in the last couple months, so there is hope that more than a few collectors will eventually own one.

Since the number of available pieces in this decal is limited, many collectors mix these items with other cadet-colored patterns such as Rose Parade and Royal Rose. All the patterns with cadet bodies go well together to create an interesting and useful collection.

"Thick Rim" bowls and casseroles have been found. This shape bowl is not as plentiful as the straight-sided bowl. The casseroles have a white lid, which contains the pattern and a blue bottom, which has no pattern.

Morning Glory Kitchenware	Price
Bowl, 6″ straight-sided	7.00-9.00
Bowl, 7½″ straight-sided	10.00-12.00
Bowl, 9″ straight-sided	14.00-16.00
Bowl, 6″ "Thick Rim"	10.00-12.00
Bowl, 7½″ "Thick Rim"	12.00-14.00

Morning Glory Kitchenware	Price
Bowl, 8½″ "Thick Rim"	14.00-16.00
Casserole, "Thick Rim"	18.00-22.00
Custard, straight-sided	8.00-10.00
Drip coffee pot, all-china	100.00-125.00
Teapot, Aladdin	35.00-45.00

Row 1: Coffee pot, all-china; teapot, Aladdin. **Row 2:** Casserole, "Thick Rim"; bowl, 7½″ "Thick Rim"; custard, straight-sided.

Rose Parade

Rose Parade kitchenware has a cadet blue body with contrasting white trim. The areas of white trim are accented by a petite pastel floral decal. The most commonly found color of the flower is pink. However, other colors which include blue and yellow may also be found. This line dates to the 1940's and has become very popular with collectors again today.

Generally, sets of Rose Parade are fairly easy to assemble. Collectors seem to be having problems finding the fluted baker, salad bowl, custard and sugar and creamer. A lid to the sugar, which would be like the red lid shown in the "Pert" section has been reported. We have not seen any blue lids, and if they exist, they are certainly the scarcest piece of Rose Parade.

Some collectors have trouble distinguishing between this pattern and another pattern with a similar pink flower on a blue body with white trim called Royal Rose. Identification has been made somewhat easier by Hall, since the majority of Rose Parade pieces contain the backstamp shown below. For pieces which may have escaped the backstamp, the Royal Rose line has silver trim and the Rose Parade pieces do not. Another confusing pink floral decal which is pictured below occasionally appears. This decal mixes well with that of Rose Parade and there is not enough of this pattern available to cause too much concern among collectors.

Kitchenware	Price	Kitchenware	Price
Baker, French fluted	25.00-28.00	Dip jar and cover, tab-handled	15.00-18.00
Bean pot, tab-handled	35.00-40.00	Jug, 5″ "Pert"	18.00-20.00
Bowl, 9″ salad	20.00-25.00	Jug, 6½″ "Pert"	20.00-25.00
Bowl, 6″ straight-sided	8.00-10.00	Jug, 7½″ "Pert"	25.00-30.00
Bowl, 7½″ straight-sided	9.00-11.00	Shakers, "Pert," ea.	7.50-8.50
Bowl, 9″ straight-sided	14.00-16.00	Sugar, "Pert"	9.00-11.00
Casserole, tab-handled	22.00-25.00	Sugar lid, "Pert"	UND
Creamer, "Pert"	10.00-12.00	Teapot, 3-cup "Pert"	22.00-25.00
Custard, straight-sided	8.00-10.00	Teapot, 6-cup "Pert"	28.00-32.00

Pink floral decal similar to Rose Parade.

Rose Parade backstamp.

Row 1: Jug, 6½″ "Pert"; jug, 5″ "Pert"; drip jar, tab-handled. **Row 2:** Bean pot, tab-handled; custard; casserole, tab-handled. **Row 3:** Teapot, 3-cup "Pert"; sugar, "Pert"; creamer, "Pert." **Row 4:** Baker, French fluted; bowl, 9″ salad.

Rose White

The Rose White kitchenware pattern features a pink rose decal on a Hi-white body with silver trim. This rose decal is the same as the decal used on blue-bodied Royal Rose pieces. However, the shape of the body of the Rose White items is the same as that in Rose Parade. The listing of Rose White pieces is not extensive, and with few exceptions, a complete set is not difficult to obtain.

The hardest pieces to find are the "Medallion" bowls, the fluted baker, the small custard and the sugar and creamer. Items easiest to get appear to be the teapots, shakers, drip jar and casserole.

In addition to the normal straight-sided bowl set, a set of bowls in the "Medallion" shape has appeared with the Rose White decal. The bottom of the bean pot will be found both with and without the rose decal. There have been no reports of a sugar lid in this pattern, but if one exists in Rose Parade, then one might also be found for this pattern.

Rose White backstamp.

Kitchenware	Price
Baker, French fluted	20.00-22.00
Bean pot, tab-handled	40.00-45.00
Bowl, 6″ "Medallion"	10.00-12.00
Bowl, 7¼″ "Medallion"	12.00-14.00
Bowl, 8½″ "Medallion"	14.00-16.00
Bowl, 6″ straight-sided	6.00-8.00
Bowl, 7½″ straight-sided	8.00-10.00
Bowl, 9″ straight-sided	10.00-12.00
Bowl, 9″ salad	15.00-18.00
Casserole, tab-handled	16.00-18.00
Creamer, "Pert"	8.00-10.00
Custard, straight-sided	7.00-9.00
Dip jar and cover, tab-handled	12.00-14.00
Jug, 5″ "Pert"	11.00-13.00
Jug, 6½″ "Pert"	13.00-15.00
Jug, 7½″ "Pert"	18.00-20.00
Shakers, "Pert," ea.	6.00-7.00
Sugar, "Pert"	8.00-10.00
Teapot, 3-cup "Pert"	18.00-20.00
Teapot, 6-cup "Pert"	25.00-30.00

Row 1: Teapot, "Pert" 6-cup; teapot, "Pert" 3-cup; mixing bowl, "Medallion." **Row 2:** Bean pot, tab-handled; jug, "Pert" 6½″ jug; "Pert" 5″. **Row 3:** Casserole, tab-handled; shaker, "Pert"; drip jar, tab-handled; shaker, "Pert."

Royal Rose

Royal Rose kitchenware has a cadet body with contrasting Hi-white features. The decoration consists of a pink rose decal and silver trim. Many people confuse this pattern with the similar blue bodied pattern–Rose Parade. However, Royal Rose pieces are accented with silver trim, and the shapes are different from those used in the Rose Parade pattern.

The Aladdin teapot and the all-china drip coffee are the most difficult items to find in Royal Rose. Also, the 9″ salad bowl, which was inadvertently omitted from the last listing, is not easily found.

Row 1: Teapot, French; Ball jug #3; teapot, Aladdin. **Row 2:** Casserole, "Thick Rim," shaker, handled; drip jar, "Thick Rim"; shaker, handled. **Row 3:** Bowl, 9″ salad; bowl, 6″ "Thick Rim"; bowl, 7½″ "Thick Rim."

Kitchenware	Price	Kitchenware	Price
Ball jug, #3	28.00-30.00	Bowl, 8½″ "Thick Rim"	14.00-16.00
Bowl, 9″ salad	18.00-20.00	Casserole, "Thick Rim"	18.00-20.00
Bowl, 6″ straight-sided	8.00-10.00	Custard, straight-sided	7.00-9.00
Bowl, 7½″ straight-sided	12.00-14.00	Drip jar and cover, "Thick Rim"	16.00-18.00
Bowl, 9″ straight-sided	16.00-18.00	Shaker, handled, ea.	8.00-9.00
Bowl, 6″ "Thick Rim"	8.00-10.00	Teapot, Aladdin	75.00-95.00
Bowl, 7½″ "Thick Rim"	10.00-12.00	Teapot, French	32.00-35.00

Shaggy Tulip

Shaggy Tulip is a colorful floral decal line dating from the mid-1930's. Not much new information concerning Shaggy Tulip has been uncovered in the three years since the last book, and only a handful of new pieces have been added to the listing. Probably the most interesting pieces to surface have been the canisters and the "Radiance" teapot. Veteran teapot collectors simply drool at the possibility of adding another teapot to their collections.

Collectors should be aware that the all-china drip cof-fee pot is one of the most common pieces of this pattern. The "Radiance" shape jug will be found with or without a cover. Keep in mind the covers are scarce, and those jugs having covers are worth about double the value of those without. Remember, the rolling pin, pie lifter, spoon, fork and dinnerware which are commonly found with this decal are not Hall items but were made by Harker. However, many enthusiasts find these are also very attractive items to display.

Row 1: Coffee pot, all-china, "Kadota"; canisters, coffee, sugar, "Radiance." **Row 2:** Jug, "Radiance"; salt and pepper, "Novelty Radiance"; custard, "Radiance."

Kitchenware	Price
Bean pot, New England #4	70.00-80.00
Canister, "Radiance"	95.00-110.00
Casserole, "Radiance"	25.00-28.00
Drip coffee pot, "Kadota" all-china	45.00-55.00
Drip jar and cover, "Radiance"	18.00-20.00
Jug and cover, "Radiance" (#2, #3)	40.00-50.00
Jug and cover, "Radiance" (#4, #5, #6)	60.00-70.00

Kitchenware	Price
Pretzel jar	75.00-85.00
Shakers, handled, ea.	8.00-9.00
Shakers, "Radiance Novelty," ea.	18.00-20.00
Shirred egg dish	18.00-20.00
Stack set, "Radiance"	45.00-55.00
Teapot, "Radiance"	100.00-125.00

Stonewall

The Stonewall decal consists of green vertical bars which look like an inverted wooden fence slat. These green bars have a white zigzag line running along each side. Positioned between the bars will be one or more green baskets of pink and orange flowers. Although most of the items in this pattern are being found with an ivory body, a few pieces have been found with an eggshell body.

The number of pieces in this listing has expanded considerably since the last book. However, none of these pieces is easy to find and anyone who chooses to collect this pattern is undertaking a considerable challenge.

Row 1: Jug, "Radiance" #5; jug, "Radiance" #2; casserole, "Radiance." **Row 2:** Leftover, square; shakers, "Novelty Radiance"; shakers, handled.

Kitchenware	Price
Casserole, "Radiance"	27.00-30.00
Drip jar, #1188 open	20.00-22.00
Drip coffee pot, all-china	100.00-125.00
Jug and cover, #2 "Radiance"	30.00-35.00
Jug and cover, #5 "Radiance"	45.00-55.00
Juicer, "Medallion"	350.00-400.00
Leftover, square	35.00-45.00
Shakers, handled (4), ea.	10.00-12.00
Shakers, "Novelty Radiance," ea.	18.00-20.00
Stack set, "Radiance"	40.00-45.00
Teapot, "Radiance"	95.00-110.00

Wild Poppy

The "Wild Poppy" decal first appeared in the late 1930's. It combines a rust-colored poppy-like flower with a sprig of wheat. This pattern was sold by Macy's, which probably explains why many of the more unusual pieces are being found in the New York area. Many items have been added to the list of known pieces in the last few years. Some of the more interesting are a number of all-china coffee pots. These may be seen in the photographs. Since the photographs were taken we have also found some "Radiance" mixing bowls with colored interiors. Some have been found with maroon interiors and others have green glaze on the inside. An abundance of casseroles and other ovenware items were also produced in this pattern. The French drip coffee biggin has been found in four-, six- and eight-cup sizes.

Row 1: Coffee pot, #691 all-china; coffee pot, Washington; canister, "Radiance" coffee; canister, "Radiance" flour. **Row 2:** Jug, "Radiance" #5; jug and cover, "Radiance" #4; jug and cover, "Radiance" #3; casserole, "Sundial" 4 ⅞". **Row 3:** Shakers, handled; shirred egg dish, 5½"; shirred egg dish, 6½". **Row 4:** Bowl, 9" "Radiance;" casserole, 10½" round; casserole, "Radiance."

Kitchenware	Price
Baker, oval	16.00-18.00
Bean pot, New England #3	65.00-75.00
Bowl, 6″ "Radiance"	10.00-12.00
Bowl, 7½″ "Radiance"	12.00-15.00
Bowl, 9″ "Radiance"	18.00-20.00
Butter dish, 1# "Zephyr"	UND
Canister, "Radiance"	95.00-125.00
Casserole, #101 oval	28.00-32.00
Casserole, #103 oval	40.00-45.00
Casserole, 8″ round 2-H	28.00-32.00
Casserole, 10½″ round	35.00-42.00
Casserole, "Radiance"	22.00-25.00
Casserole, "Sundial" #1	22.00-27.00
Casserole, "Sundial" #4	30.00-32.00
Casserole, "Thick Rim"	30.00-35.00
Coffee pot, French drip coffee biggin	85.00-95.00
Coffee pot, 12-cup Washington	60.00-65.00
Cookie jar, "Five Band"	85.00-95.00
Creamer, Hollywood	18.00-20.00
Creamer, New York	18.00-20.00
Custard, "Radiance"	6.00-8.00
Drip coffee pot, #691 all-china	95.00-110.00
Drip coffee pot, "Radiance" all-china	140.00-160.00
Drip coffee pot, sm. "Terrace"	70.00-85.00
Drip jar, "Radiance"	22.00-25.00
Jug and cover, #1, #2, #3, "Radiance"	40.00-55.00
Jug and cover, #4, #5, #6, "Radiance"	55.00-65.00
Leftover, sq.	40.00-50.00
Onion soup, individual	25.00-30.00
Shakers, handled, ea. (4)	12.00-14.00
Shakers, "Novelty Radiance"	22.00-25.00
Shakers, "Radiance" canister-style	22.00-25.00
Shirred egg dish (2 sizes)	20.00-25.00
Stack set, "Radiance"	55.00-60.00
Sugar and lid, Hollywood	22.00-25.00
Sugar and lid, New York	22.00-25.00
Teapot, French	90.00-110.00
Teapot, New York 2- or 4-cup	70.00-80.00
Teapot, New York 6- or 8-cup	80.00-95.00
Teapot, "Radiance"	95.00-110.00
Teapot, Tea for Two set	UND
Teapot, Tea for Four set	UND
Tea tile, 6″	25.00-30.00

Row 1: Coffee pot, 8-cup French coffee biggin; coffee pot, "Radiance" all-china; coffee pot, small-size "Terrace" all-china.
Row 2: Bean pot, New England #3; Stack set, "Radiance"; leftover, square. **Row 3:** Casserole, 10½″ oval; casserole, 8″ round.

Zeisel Kitchenware

In addition to the dinnerware lines which have been discussed previously, Eva Zeisel designed a kitchenware shape for Hall during the 1950's. Two patterns–Casual Living and Tri-Tone–are available.

Casual Living pieces are Seal brown and white with a decoration of pastel brushstrokes and dots in the white area.

Tri-Tone pieces have a three-color decoration–pink, turquoise and grey over a white body. The pink and turquoise areas overlap to form grey triangles and knobs of lids are also grey.

The cookie jar and the bean pot are similar in shape. The cookie jar has a flared collar into which the lid fits and the bottom is a little fatter than the bean pot bottom. The bean pot has no collar.

Kitchenware	Casual Living	Tri-Tone	Kitchenware	Casual Living	Tri-Tone
Bean pot	12.00-15.00	35.00-45.00	Creamer	3.00-4.00	6.00-8.00
Bowl, covered 2-H soup	4.00-5.00	7.00-9.00	Jam jar	3.00-4.00	9.00-11.00
Bowl, individual salad	2.00-3.00	4.00-5.00	Jug, 5 pt.	12.00-15.00	20.00-25.00
Bowl, large salad	7.00-9.00	10.00-12.00	Jug, refrigerator	15.00-18.00	45.00-50.00
Bowl, 5″		6.00-8.00	Leftover and cover	6.00-8.00	9.00-11.00
Bowl, 6″		7.00-9.00	Mug	3.00-4.00	7.00-9.00
Bowl, 7″		9.00-10.00	Relish, 1 handle	3.00-4.00	7.00-9.00
Bowl, 8″		10.00-12.00	Shakers, ea.	2.50-3.50	5.00-6.00
Bowl, 9″		12.00-15.00	Sugar and lid	3.00-4.00	8.00-10.00
Casserole, individual	4.00-6.00	10.00-12.00	Teapot, 6-cup	18.00-20.00	45.00-55.00
Casserole, oval 3 pt.	9.00-11.00	15.00-18.00	Teapot, side-handled	20.00-25.00	55.00-60.00
Casserole, oval 6 pt.	12.00-15.00	20.00-25.00	Tureen, 5 pt.	15.00-18.00	25.00-30.00
Cookie jar	12.00-15.00	35.00-45.00	Tureen, 8 pt.	20.00-25.00	35.00-40.00

Casual Living
Row 1: Tureen, 8 pt.; jug, 5 pt. **Row 2:** Creamer; sugar; relish; jam jar.

Tri-Tone
Row 1: Jug, refrigerator; jug, 5 pt.; cookie jar. **Row 2:** Teapot, side handled; teapot, 6-cup; sugar; creamer. **Row 3:** Shakers; jam jar; relish; bowl, soup (lacks cover). **Row 4:** Tureen 5 pt.; bowl, 6″; bowl, 5″. **Row 5:** Casserole, 3 pt.; casserole, 6 pt.; mug.

Miscellaneous Kitchenware

The pieces shown in the photo on the opposite page represent patterns about which very little is known at this time. In all of these patterns, we have seen less than a half dozen pieces, and in most, fewer. Some patterns have been named by researchers or collectors. We will use those names whenever possible and continue to search for answers to questions about the history of these patterns.

Row 1: The "Terrace" coffee pot and the Art Deco sugar are the same pattern. They both have the kitchenware backstamp and are decorated with an orange and yellow floral pattern. The flowers are attached to a vine-like branch with grey and brown color leaves.

The handled shakers have a bright red floral decal with dark green leaves. Both the top and bottom edges are trimmed with platinum.

The Zeisel cookie jar with the holly design was probably a seasonal item. A few other pieces with this decal have appeared. These include a coffee pot and sugar and creamer in the Coffee Set shape and a plum pudding bowl set decorated with a slighly different holly decal.

Row 2: The "Medallion" sugar and creamer are decorated with a leafy pink floral decal. A matching "Medallion" teapot is know to exist.

Pink, blue and purple flowers abound on the covered "Radiance" jug in the center of the row. This decal has also been found on a "Radiance" teapot. See the photo below.

The eggshell "Swag" shakers are from a buffet set which is usually found in the dot design. We have seen a drip jar in this pattern, but all pieces appear to be scarce. For more information on the buffet service see page 140.

Row 3: The drip jar and handled shaker with the pastel tulip pictured on the left side are similar to Shaggy Tulip.

However, they are different enough that they must be considered a separate pattern.

The "Medallion" jug in the center has a "Pink Clover" decal. A "Radiance" canister has also been found with this decal. Items with this decal bear the backstamp "Carbone, Inc." which indicates the retail store for which they were made.

The Piggly Wiggly handled shakers are from a line which Hall produced for the Piggly Wiggly grocery chain in the mid-1930's. This pattern is not easy to find, but more pieces have been showing up recently. However, it is doubtful whether enough of this pattern will ever appear to enable it to be enjoyed by more than a few determined collectors. For pieces and prices see page 165.

Row 4: The "Radiance" casserole has a greyish-white flower on what appears to be a thorny branch with brown leaves. The only other piece we know of with this decal is a "Radiance" jug.

The buffet casserole and the "Radiance" bowl have a rust color floral decal with brown leaves which collectors are calling "Autumn Flowers." Other sizes of "Radiance" bowls also may be found without too much difficulty and a square leftover has been spotted.

Row 5: The "Radiance" bowl set is the only place we have been able to find the purple and white flowers which are shown on the bowl to the left.

The "Radiance" casserole is also the only piece we know of with the floral chain decal. This decal consists of a series of white flowers suspended in a brown chain.

The decal on the bowl to the right appears to be a variation of the Red Poppy decal which might be called "Green Poppy." The decal is entirely green and the flower resembles a poppy.

Below: The daisy-like floral design on the "Radiance" canister and Drip-O-lator coffee pot has also been found on a Ball jug. The decal appears frequently on two sizes of Drip-O-lator coffee pots, but is rarely seen on the other pieces.

Piggly Wiggly	Price	Piggly Wiggly	Price
Baker, French fluted	10.00-15.00	Casserole, "Sundial"	40.00-45.00
Bean pot, New England #3	45.00-55.00	Jug, "Five Band"	16.00-20.00
Bean pot, New England #4	50.00-60.00	Marmite, petite	20.00-25.00
Casserole, "Five Band"	30.00-35.00	Shaker, handled, ea.	10.00-12.00
Casserole, "Radiance"	30.00-35.00	Stack set, "Radiance"	45.00-55.00

Handpainted Kitchenware

Many, but not all, hand-decorated pieces were decorated by artists at Hall. Pictured below are some artist decorated pieces and a child's New York creamer with an animal decal.

		Price
Row 1:	Carafe, signed "Jean Alpert"	85.00-95.00
	Cookie jar, signed "Kay '79"	65.00-75.00
	Syrup, "Sundial," signed "Elita"	45.00-55.00
	Creamer, New York with children's decal	25.00-35.00
Row 2:	Teapot, Aladdin, signed "E.L. Cross"	125.00-150.00
	Shakers, handled, signed "Edith Payment"	20.00-30.00
	Teapot, Boston, signed "Edith Payment"	90.00-110.00

Hall Radiant Ware

Hall produced a set of four bowls for the Jewel Tea Company in the 1940's. The brightly colored bowls are known as the "Rainbow" bowl set and have the following backstamp: "Hall Radiant Ware." Each bowl will be found in a single color.

Bowl	Price
Red	10.00-12.00
Blue	7.00-9.00
Yellow	6.00-8.00
Green	7.00-9.00

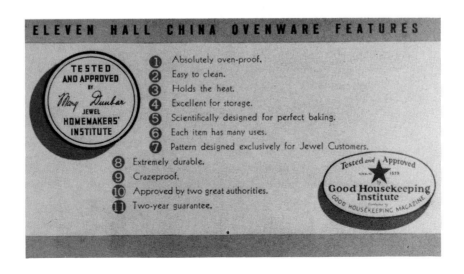

Red Kitchenware

		Price			Price
Row 1:	Pretzel jar	50.00-60.00	**Row 3:**	Sugar and creamer, "Norse"	18.00-22.00
	Coffee pot, "Baron"	32.00-35.00		Petite Marmite	7.00-9.00
	Tea for Two set	60.00-70.00		Ashtray	8.00-10.00
	Vase, #641	10.00-12.00		Bean Pot, New England	35.00-45.00
Row 2:	Water server, #628	40.00-45.00	**Row 4:**	Teapot, Morning Set	35.00-45.00
	Water server, Plaza	35.00-45.00		Covered sugar, Morning Set	9.00-11.00
	Shakers, handled with embossed			Creamer, Morning Set	9.00-11.00
	letters, ea.	7.00-9.00		Trivet	6.00-8.00

Part III: Refrigerator Ware

The popularity of the modern electric refrigerator in the late 1930's resulted in the production of numerous types of cold storage units from glass and china. Hall China made items for retail sale as well as exclusive designs for Westinghouse, General Electric, Sears, Hotpoint and Montgomery Ward. Premium-type refrigerator items were also an important part of the production of the era. The accompanying McCormick reprint illustrates an example of one such premium.

Three basic items are included in the Hall refrigerator line. They are water bottles or water servers, leftovers or refrigerator boxes and covered butters.

The water containers are covered pieces intended to be placed in the refrigerator for water storage. Closure is achieved with either a cork-encased china stopper or with a china lid. Leftovers are deep dishes with a shallow or flat china lid. The butter dishes have a flat bottom and a deep lid.

Today the popularity of Hall refrigerator ware is astounding. Many people are again using these items in their refrigerators and the water servers are especially popular. The renewed interest in Hall water servers may have been partly responsible for Hall's re-introduction of the Streamline and "Norris" shapes for the retail market a few years ago.

Westinghouse

The "Hercules" shape was offered as "Peasant Ware" by Westinghouse in 1940 and 1941. A set consisted of a rectangular butter, a water server and two leftovers. Cobalt is the most common color of the water server, but it may also be found in tan with the Westinghouse backstamp. Later, this mold was used to produce water servers in cobalt, tan, brown and ivory. Most of these will have the "TOUCAN ENTERPRISES, CHICAGO" backstamp. Currently, this covered water server is being produced in several colors as part of the Hall American line. To identify the new pieces look for the post 1970 square backstamp. In addition to the regular split-lid shape water server another style has been found. The second shape, which has a full-length, detached, semi-hinged lid is shown in the photo below.

The "General" design was offered in 1939 as an accessory to Westinghouse refrigerators. Sets were comprised of a water server, two leftovers and a butter. The water server is found frequently in delphinium, and has been showing up with some regularity in garden green. The butter and leftovers are usually seen in garden, sunset, delphinium and yellow.

"Phoenix" was the earliest line of Hall refrigerator ware used by Westinghouse. This line was introduced in 1938 and consisted of a water server, a leftover and a butter. The most commonly found color is delphinium, but all three pieces are also found occasionally in lettuce green. There have also been reports of a cobalt water server.

The "Adonis" line in blue and daffodil was offered by Westinghouse in 1952. A set consisted of a water server, four small round leftovers and two rectangular leftovers. Two styles of ovenware sets were offered at the same time. These pieces are shown at the top of page 173. Each set consisted of three pieces–two covered casseroles and one open baker. The "Ridged" line came in canary and the "Plain" line was made in delphinium.

Refrigerator Ware	"Hercules"	"General"	"Phoenix"	"Adonis"
Butter	10.00-12.00	10.00-12.00	9.00-11.00	
Leftover, rect.	6.00-7.00	7.00-8.00	6.00-7.00	7.00-9.00
Leftover, round				5.00-6.00
Water server with lid	45.00-55.00*	22.00-27.00	22.00-27.00	20.00-25.00

*Currently part of the Hall American line

Bakeware	"Ridged"	"Plain"
Casserole, covered	10.00-12.00	10.00-12.00
Baker, open	6.00-7.00	6.00-7.00

Hinged-lid "Hercules" water server.

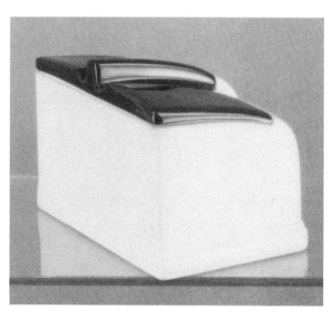

Black and white Sears' leftover.

Row 1: Water Server, "Hercules"; water server, "Hercules"; leftover, "Hercules"; butter, "Hercules." **Row 2:** Leftover, "General"; butter, "General"; water server, "General." **Row 3:** Water server, "Phoenix"; leftover, "Phoenix"; butter, "Phoenix." **Row 4:** Leftover, rectangular, "Adonis"; water server, "Adonis"; leftover, small round, "Adonis."

Montgomery Ward, Hotpoint, Sears, General Electric

Hall produced a line of refrigerator ware for Montgomery Ward in the early 1940's. The color usually seen is delphinium, but pieces can also be found in the midwhite color. There are two styles of rectangular leftover.

Refrigerator Ware	Price
Bowl, sm. covered	10.00-12.00
Bowl, med. covered	12.00-14.00
Bowl, lg. covered	14.00-16.00
Bowl, knob handle	12.00-14.00
Butter	20.00-22.00
Leftover, rect.	8.00-10.00
Leftover, lg. rect.	18.00-20.00
Water server with lid	22.00-27.00

The larger one with the V-shape lid is not easy to find. Also included in the set are three sizes of round, covered bowls with raised elongated handles, a rectangular butter and a water server.

Brightly colored leftovers were included in a refrigerator ware line which Hall produced for Hotpoint. The line consisted of a water server, three round leftovers, five square leftovers and a rectangular leftover. The water servers with the cork encased china stoppers are not easy to find. Some sizes of the square leftovers and the rectangular leftover are also proving hard to find. For some reason, many dealers think the presence of the Hotpoint insignia on these pieces automatically makes them a "rare" advertising collectible. Some leftovers we have seen have been priced as museum pieces rather than as a common collectible.

Refrigerator Ware	Price
Leftover, rect.	10.00-12.00
Leftover, 6¾″ round	8.00-10.00
Leftover, 7¾″ round	12.00-14.00
Leftover, 8¾″ round	16.00-18.00
Leftover, 4″ sq.	7.00-9.00
Leftover, 4¾″ sq.	10.00-12.00
Leftover, 5¾″ sq.	10.00-12.00
Leftover, 6¾″ sq.	16.00-18.00
Leftover, 8½″ sq.	20.00-22.00
Water server with lid	27.00-30.00

Hall made one piece of refrigerator ware for Sears. It is a three-part leftover which is normally found in the cadet and Hi-white colors. The center piece is solid cadet and the end pieces have cadet bases and Hi-white lids.

There have been several reports of another color combination being found. This set has a solid Hi-black center piece and Hi-white end pieces which have Hi-black lids. An example of the end section is shown on page 170.

	Price
Sears' leftover, 3-part	27.00-32.00

Hall modified its Westinghouse "Adonis" line for use with General Electric refrigerators. The GE logo was used on the lids and the new colors were addison and daffodil. Two new pieces were added–a handled casserole and a large round leftover.

General Electric	Price
Casserole	12.00-14.00
Leftover, rect.	8.00-10.00
Leftover, sm. round	3.00-4.00
Leftover, lg. round	9.00-11.00
Water server with lid	20.00-25.00

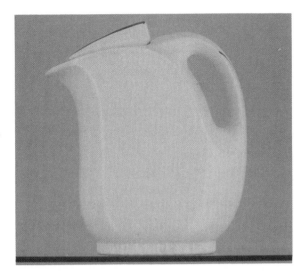

Montgomery Ward water server, white with red trim.

Row 1: Casserole, covered, "Ridged" Westinghouse; baker, open "Ridged" Westinghouse; casserole, covered, "Plain" Westinghouse. **Row 2:** Leftover, rectangular, Montgomery Ward; bowl, covered, Montgomery Ward; water server, Montgomery Ward; leftover, large rectangular, Montgomery Ward. **Row 3:** Water server, Hotpoint; leftover, 8½" square, Hotpoint; leftover 6¾" round, Hotpoint. **Row 4:** Leftover, 3-section, Sears. **Row 5:** Water server, General Electric; casserole, General Electric; leftover rectangular, General Electric.

Miscellaneous Refrigerator Ware

Hall made numerous shapes of refrigerator ware for the retail market. Some of these shapes are still in the current line and are being sold at department stores and specialty shops around the country.

The Ball jug was introduced in 1938, and quickly became a best seller for Hall. It may be found in numerous solid colors and is in virtually all the decal lines. It is available in four different sizes–1½ pt., 2⅓ pt., 2 qt. and 5¼ pt. The #3 size, 2 quart, is the most commonly found size. Although this shape was not chosen for reissue in the Hall American line, new ball jugs in stock green and stock brown are available in the institutional line.

The "Nora" water servers came with and without china lids. They were a covered water server available in Hall's general line and also were a premium item for McCormick Tea in their lidless form. See the reprint from a 1955 magazine at the front of this section. New covered jugs in this shape are currently being produced for the Hall American line.

The Donut jug was introduced in the late 1930's and is still in the institutional line. This jug was also reissued in 1984 as a part of Hall's re-entry into the retail market. The old Donut jug may be found in two sizes and a variety of solid colors. It has also been found in a few of the decal lines and some have been appearing with gold decoration. The green one in the picture has the gold

"French Flower" decoration along with a gold encrusted handle and gold around the lip.

The loop handle jug was introduced in the 1930's and is still available in the general line. It was made in two sizes and is found in many different solid colors and a few of the decal lines. The smaller size appears to be harder to find than the larger size.

The Plaza water server may be found with a cork encased china stopper, but so many of these jugs have been found without stoppers that they were probably issued without them in some promotion. Although the jug was produced from the 1930's to the 1960's, not many are being found today.

The Streamline jug was selected for reissue in the Hall American line. The older jugs are not easy to find and date to the 1930's. New pieces will bear the square backstamp.

The #628 water server has been found in numerous colors. It was introduced in the late 1930's, but is no longer in production.

The "Zephyr" line consists of two sizes of stoppered water bottles, a covered one-pound butter and a covered rectangular leftover. The line dates to the late 1930's and will be found predominantly in the Chinese red color. However, pieces do exist in a few of the decal lines, and recently, a blue water bottle was discovered. Pictured below are the two sizes of water bottles.

Refrigerator Ware	Price
Ball jug #1, 5¼"	18.00-25.00
Ball jug #2, 5¾"	18.00-25.00
Ball jug #3, 7"	15.00-22.00
Ball jug #4, 7½"	22.00-27.00
Donut jug, large	20.00-30.00
Donut jug, small	25.00-32.00
Loop handle jug, large	18.00-27.00
Loop handle jug, small	25.00-30.00
#628 water server	40.00-45.00

Refrigerator Ware	Price
*"Nora" water server	10.00-12.00
*Plaza water server	35.00-45.00
Streamline jug	35.00-40.00
"Zephyr" butter	65.00-75.00
"Zephyr" leftover	40.00-45.00
"Zephyr" water bottle (2 sizes)	55.00-60.00

*With lids, double price

"Zephyr" water bottles.

Row 1: Ball jug #3; Ball jug #3; "Nora" water server. **Row 2:** Donut jug; Donut jug with gold "French Flower" decoration; loop handle jug. **Row 3:** Plaza water server; Streamline jug; #628 water server. **Row 4:** "Zephyr" water bottle; "Zephyr" butter; "Zephyr" leftover.

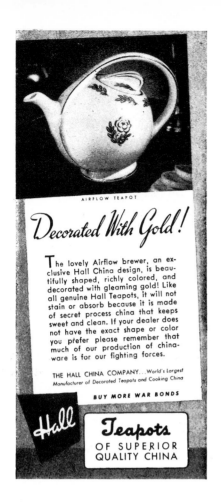
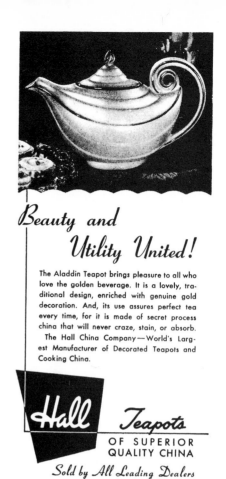

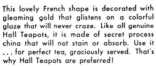

Part IV: Teapots and Coffee Pots

The first Hall teapots were part of the institutional line. The early colors were stock brown, stock green and white. In 1920, the Boston, New York and French shapes were selected for a store promotion. These teapots were decorated with gold and Hall's Gold Decorated Teapot line was born. The new line was very successful and many new shapes were added over the next few decades. These new shapes were combined with a rainbow of new colors to catapult Hall China into prominence as the leading producer of teapots in the world.

Many of Hall's teapots, which are collectible today, are part of the Gold Decorated line. The backstamp on these teapots will usually include a gold code number which was used for reordering purposes. Each shape teapot will have a standard gold design, although some experimentation in the early years has resulted in different gold designs on some of the older teapots. Also, on some shapes there is a gold decoration which collectors refer to as "special." "Specials" have the standard gold design for their shape. In addition, they also will have gold encrusted handles, spouts and knobs of the lids. The gold mark on the backstamp will usually be followed by an "S."

Undecorated teapots will usually have the #3 backstamp. Red teapots have the #4 kitchenware backstamp and teapots made in the 1920's or early 1930's have the #2 backstamp.

In the 1930's, six teapots were selected for decal decoration. Shapes which were chosen are the Baltimore, French, Los Angeles, Newport, New York and Philadelphia. Sales of these teapots with the decal decorations were not very good. Therefore, most of them are difficult for collectors to find.

In the early 1940's, Hall introduced a series of six teapots which has become known as the Victorian line. Although several of these teapots have been found in two colors, they were essentially only offered in one basic color. Later, gold decoration was added in an attempt to increase sales. However, this line was never very popular, and it was discontinued by the end of the decade.

Also in the 1940's, another series of six teapots, called the Brilliant Series, was designed by J. Palin Thorely. These teapots were made in several colors, but each style has a single color in which it will be found most often. Decorations included rhinestones, decals and gold, but many of these teapots will also be found undecorated. This line was offered sporadically through the late 1960's.

In the late 1950's, Hall brought out a new line of teapots called Gold Label. These teapots were very gaudy–almost covered with gold decoration. The shapes of the teapots were selected from among those used earlier. No new shapes were introduced. This new line of teapots was sold along with several other matching kitchenware accessories. Gold Label decorated teapots may be identified through the letters "GL" which follow the gold code number on the bottom of the teapots.

In the 1960's another attempt was made to revive the interest in teapots through the use of decals. The six teapots chosen and their decorations are as follows:

Teapot	Decoration
Boston	gold fruit decal
French	gold rose decal
Hollywood	gold leaf decal
Los Angeles	green & yellow leaf decal
Philadelphia	black hearth scene decal
Windshield	green, white & brown floral blend

Today, Hall is again offering teapots to the public through retail outlets via their Hall American line. The Airflow, Rhythm and square T-Ball teapots are being marketed through major department stores and specialty shops across the country. To identify these new issues, look for the square backstamp.

Hall produced many different coffee pots. A lot of these pots were used in the decal lines and will be identified there. However, some were sold to other companies such as Enterprise, Tricolator and Westinghouse. These companies then added the metal parts and marketed the finished product. Some, but not all of the coffee pots will bear a Hall backstamp.

To help with identification, the coffee pots and teapots in the following photographs will have both their shape name and color name. In some cases recognition of the colors may still be difficult since some colors do not print the exact shade. Since color is such an important factor in the price of the teapots, an attempt will be made to note the hard-to-find colors for each shape. The price guide has been divided into as many categories as practical to aid collectors in their attempt to distinguish between common and unusual teapots.

Novelty Teapots

The automobile is a six-cup novelty teapot which was introduced in 1938. The unique styling of this teapot continuously amazes spectators at glass and pottery shows today. Even unenlightened browsers are impressed by the lines of this unusual teapot, and that is even before they find out the price. The automobile may be found in a number of solid colors. Red, cobalt, maroon, canary and turquoise appear to be most common. Also, it may be found in many of these same colors with either gold or platinum trim. The decorated teapots usually have an encrusted spout, solid decoration on the raised areas of the lid, and highlighted wheels, fenders and door hinges and handles. However, some teapots will be found with a decoration which consists of merely a few simple gold or platinum lines. Although this teapot is still highly collectible, an ample supply has surfaced in the last several years to result in a fairly stable price–especially for the more commonly found colors.

The basket is a six-cup teapot which was first made in 1938. It is the easiest to find of all the novelty teapots. Baskets are usually found in canary and will be commonly decorated with a few platinum lines. The most easily found undecorated colors are Chinese red and canary. The basket will also be found in other colors, but these are rather unusual.

The basketball has consistently proven to be the hardest to find of the novelty teapots. It is a six-cup teapot which first made its appearance in 1938. However, it has not surpassed the football or automobile in desirability or price. The most commonly found colors are undecorated Chinese red and decorated turquoise. The decorated basketball in the picture is what collectors call a special since it has a gold encrusted handle and spout in addition to the standard decoration.

The birdcage is a hard-to-find novelty teapot which was introduced in 1939. It will be found in solid colors and with gold decoration. Gold decoration consists of highlighting lines on the cage and gold decoration on the embossed birds. The most commonly found undecorated color is Chinese red. Decorated birdcages are turning up most often in maroon, blue and emerald green.

The donut, which first appeared in 1938, is one of the easiest to find of all the novelty teapots. However, phenomenal collector demand has kept the price high and the supply low. Gold decoration consists of a few simple lines accenting the handle, spout and lid. The donut is found in a variety of solid colors and is the only novelty teapot which has been found in the dinnerware decal patterns. It is found most often with the Orange Poppy decal and is also known to exist in the Crocus pattern.

The football seems to be appearing more frequently lately than it has in the past. Maybe its high price is forcing some out of attics. However, collector enthusiasm for these teapots is keeping the price high and the supply of all mint condition teapots is being quickly absorbed into collections. The football has been found in numerous solid colors. Of these red, cobalt, maroon and turquoise are probably the most common. gold decoration normally consists of a few simple lines on the handle, lid and side of the teapot. However, a variation dubbed a "special" will be found which has a gold encrusted handle and spout in addition to the standard gold lines.

Teapot	Introduced	Red/Cobalt*	Other Colors*
Automobile	1938	350.00-400.00	300.00-350.00
Basket	1938	90.00-110.00	40.00-55.00
Basketball	1938	350.00-390.00	300.00-350.00
Birdcage	1938	300.00-350.00	165.00-195.00
Donut	1938	125.00-150.00	115.00-135.00
Football	1938	350.00-390.00	300.00-350.00

* Gold or silver decoration, add 10%

Row 1: Automobile, cobalt; automobile, canary/gold;automobile, maroon/platinum. **Row 2:** Basket, canary/platinum; basketball, turquoise/gold; basketball, Chinese red. **Row 3:** Birdcage, maroon/gold; birdcage, cadet; donut, cobalt. **Row 4:** Donut, ivory; football, cobalt; football, cobalt/gold.

Airflow Teapot

The Airflow teapot was introduced in 1940 and was produced in eight-cup and six-cup sizes. Today, the larger eight-cup size is much harder to find than the smaller version. The Airflow will be found in a variety of solid colors. The most commonly found colors are cobalt, canary and Chinese red. In addition, a standard gold decoration and several variations of the standard decoration will be found. The standard decoration consists of a large single rose on the center of each side of the teapot and multiple gold leaf sprigs around the opening. The foot, handle and lid are accented with gold lines. All the teapots in the picture except the cobalt and red ones have the standard decoration. A variation of the gold decoration includes a "special" which may be seen on the cobalt teapot shown on the top row. This consists of a gold encrusted handle and spout used in combination with the standard decoration. Other variations are achieved by deleting a part of the standard decoration. One version omits the large center rose on the sides of the teapot. Another style omits both the flowers and leaves, leaving only the thin gold highlighting lines. The only reports of any Airflow teapots appearing with decals have been in the Blue Blossom and Blue Garden patterns.

The Airflow teapot was one of the items Hall chose to re-introduce in 1985 when the retail business was re-established. New Airflow teapots will be found, but all should have the square backstamp which has been in use since the 1970's. Also, at this writing, new gold decorated teapots have not been produced.

Row 1: Airflow, 8-cup emerald/standard gold; Airflow, 8-cup maroon/standard gold; Airflow, 6-cup cobalt/gold "special." **Row 2:** Airflow, 6-cup cadet/standard gold; Airflow, 6-cup Chinese red; Airflow, 6-cup marine/standard gold.

Teapot	Red/Cobalt	Canary/ Turquoise	Other Solid Colors	Gold Decorated "Special"
Airflow, 6-cup	35.00-40.00	20.00-25.00	27.00-32.00	35.00-40.00
Airflow, 8-cup	37.00-45.00	25.00-30.00	30.00-35.00	35.00-40.00

Standard gold decorated prices are the same as for solid colors.

Aladdin Teapots

The original thin style Aladdin teapot with the round opening was introduced in 1939. In 1940, an optional infusor was offered. A few years later Hall experimented with an Aladdin teapot with an oval opening and an oval lid and infusor. However, by the end of World War II the teapot with the round opening was reinstated. In 1942, a modified wide-bodied version of the Aladdin teapot was introdcued to be used with Jewel's Autumn and Morning Glory patterns. For the most part, very few other patterns or decorations will be found on this style of teapot. However, there are some exceptions as can be seen in the photo on the next page. The hand painted teapot and the one with the floral basket decal feature the wide-body Aladdin.

Undecorated Aladdin teapots may be found in almost any Hall color. There are several variations of gold decorated Aladdin teapots. The simplest decoration consists of thin gold lines highlighting the handle, spout, lid opening, lid base and knob. Examples are shown on the

blue and chartreuse teapots in the top row. The yellow teapot on the second row is an example of a Gold Label decoration called "squiggle." Colors available are daffodil and ivory. For other matching pieces in this pattern see page 148. The heavily gold encrusted pink and maroon teapots are also part of the Gold Label line. The design on these teapots is called "Swag." Other colors which are sometimes found with this design include ivory and marine.

The yellow teapot with gold blobs, shown in the photo on the next page, appears to have been decorated with a sponge. This is one of the more gaudy and unusually decorated Aladdin teapots. The turquoise teapot on the bottom row with the gold handle and the gold knob on the lid is what is referred to as a "special." A variation of these "specials" will be found with a gold encrusted spout. This teapot also features the much scarcer oval opening. Notice the accompanying sugar and creamer in the Boston shape which completes this set.

Row 1: Aladdin, matte black and white with satin gold; Aladdin, chartreuse/gold; Aladdin, turquoise blue/gold. **Row 2:** Aladdin, daffodil, Gold label, "Squiggle" design; Aladdin, pink, Gold Label, "Swag" design; Aladdin, maroon, Gold Label "swag" design.

Row 1: Aladdin, ivory with floral basket decal; Aladdin, canary with gold spatter; Aladdin, ivory, hand-painted, artist signed. **Row 2:** Aladdin turquoise, "special" gold decoration with matching Boston shape sugar and creamer.

A multitude of regular-style Aladdin teapots will be found with decals. Some of the more common ones are in the Blue Bouquet, Red Poppy and Wildfire patterns. Other patterns where the Aladdin teapot is a rarity include Crocus, Blue Blossom, Blue Garden and Brown-Eyed Susan. For more information on the availability and prices of Aladdin teapots with decals, see the individual dinnerware and kitchenware listings.

	Red Cobalt*	Other Solid Colors*	Gold Label
Aladdin, oval opening	40.00-45.00	18.00-25.00	-----
Aladdin, round opening	35.00-40.00	18.00-22.00	35.00-40.00

* Gold decorated, add 10%
Handpainted or very unusual gold decoration, 60.00-90.00

1. French, 6-cup ivory, gold Label "daisy" decoration; **2.** French, 4-cup cadet, Gold Label "daisy" decoration; **3.** French, 3-cup, cobalt with gold band. **4.** French, 2-cup stock brown, French flower decoration. **5.** French, 2-cup canary.

Bellvue and French Teapots

Interest in the Bellvue teapot among many collectors has been minimal. The teapot was introduced in the 1920's, will be found in at least six different sizes and is still being made in some colors. It is commonly found in stock brown and stock green, but as can be seen in the photo, it will occasionally be found in attractive colors and with gold decoration. It has been found in one decal line in the 2-cup size–Orange Poppy–and attracts great collector interest among those interested in that pattern.

The French teapot was one of the earliest to be added to the Gold Decorated Line. This style teapot is a perfect example of Hall's decorating diversity. The gold decorations on some of the early teapots exhibit excellent craftsmanship. A prime example is the cobalt teapot with the gold palm leaf decoration which is shown in the photograph. Some of the early teapots dating from the 1920's, such as the two cobalt ones pictured, will be found with infusors. Later French teapots do not have infusors. The two most frequently found gold decorations are the "daisy" from the Gold Label line and the gold flower decoration like the one shown on the 2-cup stock brown teapot. These two decorations are found on all sizes of French teapots ranging from the 1-cup size to the 12-cup size. The various sizes of the French teapot which have been found are 1-, 1½-, 2-, 3-, 4-, 6-, 8-, 10- and 12-cups. The six- and eight-cup sizes of French teapots are the most common. The six-cup teapot will also be found in numerous colors with Lipton Tea embossed in the bottom. Boston shape sugars and creamers will also be found to match these teapots in most colors. The matte black six-cup teapot with the gold rose decal to the left on the second shelf was sold by Sears during the 1960's.

Row 1: Bellvue, 2-cup cobalt/gold; French, 6-cup ivory with embossed gold band decoration; French 4-cup with infusor and standard New York gold decoration; French, 4-cup ivory with handpainted Nouveau decoration. **Row 2:** French, 6-cup matte black with Sears gold rose decal; French 8-cup cobalt with gold palm leaf decoration and matching Boston shape sugar and creamer.

Teapot	Common Solid Colors*	Cobalt/ Red	Old Gold Decorated	Gold Label
Bellvue, 2-4 cup	8.00-10.00	25.00-30.00		
Bellvue, 6-10 cup	12.00-18.00	30.00-35.00		
French, 1-3 cup	10.00-15.00	30.00-35.00	35.00-45.00	25.00-30.00
French, 4-6 cup	12.00-16.00	30.00-35.00	35.00-45.00	25.00-30.00
French, 8-12 cup	18.00-22.00	35.00-40.00	40.00-47.50	27.00-32.00

* Stock Brown or Stock Green, 8.00-12.00.
Bellvue, gold decorated, 25.00-35.00.
French, gold palm leaf decoration, 65.00-75.00.

Globe, Hook Cover, Manhattan, World's Fair, Melody

The six-cup Globe teapot was made with two different shapes of spouts. The No-Drip spout Globe shown on the top row has a different standard gold decoration than the regular Globe pictured on the second row. Both teapots are found more often with gold decoration than without. Both styles are hard to find, but the No-Drip version appears to be a little more available than the other style.

The Hook Cover is a six-cup teapot which was introduced in 1940. It derives its name from the small hook on the body over which an opening in the lid fits to lock it into place. Colors usually found are cadet and delphinium. The standard gold decoration consists of a large gold flower along with four gold sprigs on each side of the body and gold trim on the foot, spout, handle and around the lid and lid opening. The Gold Label version of the Hook Cover is covered with gold stars and sports a gold encrusted handle and spout.

The side-handle Manhattan teapot is usually found in the small two-cup size. It is most frequently seen in stock brown, maroon and cobalt, and we have not seen this teapot decorated.

The World's Fair teapot was a promotional item for the 1940 New York World's Fair. It incorporated a gold trylon and perisphere on a cobalt body of the Star shape. Most have the following backstamp: "A GENUINE HALL TEAPOT--MADE IN U.S.A.--SOLD EXCLUSIVELY AT THE NEW YORK WORLD'S FAIR--1940" A few teapots have been found with a 1939 date in the backstamp.

The Melody teapot was first produced in 1939. It is a six-cup teapot which may be found with gold decoration; although it is probably found more frequently without decoration. The standard gold design on the body is three rings close to the base and three more rings inside the white collar in addition to trim on the handle and around the top edge. The lid is also decorated with a gold ring. The Melody is also sometimes found decorated with the Orange Poppy decal.

Star-shaped teapot with World's Fair Decoration.

Teapot	Red/Cobalt*	Other Colors*	Gold Label
Globe	60.00-65.00	45.00-55.00	
Globe, No-Drip	60.00-65.00	45.00-55.00	
Hook Cover	32.00-37.00	16.00-18.00	18.00-22.00
Manhattan	37.00-45.00	30.00-37.00	
World's Fair	285.00-330.00		
Melody	85.00-95.00	65.00-75.00	

* Gold decorated price the same as solid colors.

Row 1: Globe No-Drip, marine with standard gold decoration; Globe No-Drip, Monterrey with standard gold decoration; Globe No-Drip, Addison with standard gold decoration. **Row 2:** Globe, cobalt with standard gold decoration; Globe, turquoise; Hook Cover, cobalt. **Row 3:** Side-handle Manhattan, cobalt; side-handle Manhattan, stock brown; World's Fair Star, cobalt. **Row 4:** Melody, cobalt with standard gold decoration; Melody, Chinese red.

Moderne, Nautilus, Parade, Rhythm and "Sundial"

The Moderne teapot has a six-cup capacity. It is commonly found in ivory, canary and cadet, and is usually seen without gold decoration. The standard gold application is limited to the knob of the lid, the very inside tip of the spout and the foot. The plain design of this teapot has caused many common color Moderne teapots to be left on dealer's tables begging for homes.

The Nautilus is a sea shell-shaped six-cup teapot which first appeared in 1939. This teapot is hard to find and commands a respectable price. Normal gold decoration is limited to a few simple lines as may be seen on the turquoise teapot in the photo.

The parade is a common six-cup teapot which is usually found in canary. The standard gold decoration is illustrated in the photograph. Finding colors such as red, maroon or cobalt is a challenge, but not an impossible task. The Parade teapot is also part of the Gold Label line. The most commonly found color of the Gold Label teapot is also canary and the gold design is Squiggle.

The Rhythm is a six-cup teapot which was introduced in 1939. Due to the design of the teapot, it is very difficult to find this piece with a good lid. The standard gold decoration is pictured and easiest color to find is canary.

The "Sundial" teapot is usually seen in canary. The standard gold decoration is shown on the canary teapot in the picture. This shape teapot is a basic part of one of Hall's major kitchenware shapes and will also be found with several decal decorations. The "Sundial" teapot was also made in the 8 oz. and 10 oz. individual sizes. These sizes are still being made in stock green and stock brown.

Row 1: Moderne, ivory/gold; Nautilus, Chinese red; Nautilus, cobalt/gold. **Row 2:** Parade, canary/gold; Parade, cobalt/gold; Rhythm, Monterrey/gold. **Row 3:** "Sundial" cobalt; "Sundial," canary/gold; "Sundial," Blue Blossom decal; "Sundial," 2-cup marine.

Teapot	Red/Cobalt	Common Colors	Unusual Colors	Gold Label
Moderne		14.00-16.00	18.00-20.00	
Nautilus	95.00-110.00	60.00-70.00	75.00-95.00	
Parade	45.00-55.00	12.00-14.00	35.00-45.00	20.00-22.00
Rhythm	95.00-110.00	40.00-45.00	65.00-75.00	
"Sundial"	55.00-65.00	40.00-45.00	45.00-55.00	

Star and Streamline Teapots

The Star teapot has been named for its commonly found style of decoration. It was introduced in 1939 and is only available in the six-cup size. Turquoise and cobalt are the only common colors. Other decorated colors will be found with diligent searching. Also, undecorated versions of this teapot were made. Again, the most abundant undecorated colors are turquoise and cobalt. The 1939 and 1940 New York World's Fair logo will appear on the bottom of some cobalt Star teapots. Either date may be found and the World's Fair trylon and perisphere will be found on the side of these cobalt teapots. The 1939 date is the hardest to find, but both of these teapots are unusual.

The Streamline is a six-cup teapot which first appeared in 1937. It is commonly found in canary, delphinium and Chinese red. Gold decoration most often consists of a few narrow lines outlining the lid opening, handle, spout, lid and knob. However, a "special" gold decoration exists which features a gold encrusted handle, spout and knob. This may be seen on the yellow teapot in the photo. A platinum decoration has also been found on some canary teapots. The platinum bands are much wider and more gaudy than the standard gold lines. The Streamline shape is also used in a number of the decal lines.

Row 1: Star, turquoise/gold; Star, cobalt/gold; Streamline, emerald. **Row 2:** Streamline, canary with "special" gold decoration; Streamline, delphinium/gold; Streamline, Chinese red.

Teapot	Red/Cobalt	Common Colors	Unusual Colors
Star		25.00-30.00	45.00-55.00
World's Fair	285.00-330.00		
Streamline	35.00-40.00	18.00-20.00	30.00-35.00*

* With "special" gold decoration, 45.00-50.00.

Surfside and Windshield Teapots

The Surfside teapot has a six-cup capacity and was introduced in 1937. It is usually found with the standard gold decoration shown on the canary teapot in the picture. However, it may also be found in various solid colors without decoration or with the "special" gold decoration as seen on the emerald green teapot in the photo. "Special" teapots such as this were often sold in sets with an accompanying sugar and creamer. In this case the matching sugar and creamer set is the Boston shape. The most readily found colors are emerald and canary. The Surfside has not been found in any of the decal patterns.

The six-cup Windshield teapot was first offered in 1941. The colors easiest to find are camellia, maroon and the ivory Gold Label with polka dots. This style teapot is available both with and without gold decoration and will also be found in some of the decal patterns. The standard Windshield gold floral decoration is shown on the maroon teapot. The Gold Label teapot also has matching kitchenware accessories which include a cookie jar, casserole and three-piece bowl set. The yellow teapot is from a decal line Hall experimented with in the 1960's. Several game bird decals will be found on ivory Windshield teapots. These include scenes with ducks, pheasants and grouse.

Row 1: Surfside, canary/gold; Surfside, emerald with "special" gold decoration. **Row 2:** Windshield, ivory with pheasant decal; Windshield, yellow with brown, green and white floral band; Windshield, ivory Gold Label polka dot; Windshield, maroon/gold.

Teapot	Common Color	Unusual Color	Gold Label	Special
Surfside	35.00-40.00	55.00-65.00		75.00-85.00
Windshield*	15.00-18.00	35.00-45.00†	18.00-22.00	

* With game bird decal, 65.00-75.00.
  With Carrot or Clover decal, 45.00-55.00.
†Cobalt with gold, add 50 percent

Albany Teapots

The six-cup Albany teapot was introduced in the early 1930's. It will be found undecorated and with three different gold decorations. The color seen most frequently with the standard decoration is turquoise.

The three different styles of gold decorations are shown in the photograph. The turquoise blue and emerald teapots depict the standard Albany gold decoration. The "special" variation is illustrated by the cobalt teapot. This includes the standard decoration and a gold encrusted handle, spout and knob on the lid. The teapots in the second row are examples of the two colors associated with the Gold Label line.

Common and less collectible colors: All greens, all browns, pink, black, ivory, turquoise and most lighter blues.

Unusual and more collectible colors: Cobalt, rose, warm yellow, canary, maroon, orchid and grey.

Row 1: Albany, turquoise blue/standard gold; Albany, emerald/standard gold; Albany, cobalt with "special" gold decoration. **Row 2:** Albany, mahogany Gold Label; Albany, pink Gold Label.

Teapot	Common Color	Unusual Color	Gold Label	Gold Special
Albany	20.00-25.00	35.00-45.00	35.00-45.00	45.00-55.00

Baltimore and Boston Teapots

The Baltimore teapot holds six-cups and first appeared in the early 1930's. It may be found undecorated, with several styles of gold decorations, or with different decals. Colors which are easiest to find include maroon, emerald and marine. The cadet teapot in the picture is an example of the standard gold decoration. The maroon teapot is from the Gold Label Line. Although the Baltimore teapot has not been found as a part of the regular decal dinnerware or kitchenware lines, this teapot has been found with several interesting decals. One decal, shown in this picture, features multiple pink roses on an ivory body. Another decal, Minuet, is usually found on a warm yellow teapot. An example of this decal may be seen on a Philadelphia teapot, pictured on page 199.

The Boston shape teapot was one of the original four teapots selected for Hall's venture into the retail markets in 1920. During the 1920's several different styles of gold decoration were used. These early decorations are not easy to find today, but are seen most often on teapots with a cobalt body. Look for the embossed HALL mark used in combination with the #2 backstamp to help identify these early teapots.

The decoration shown on the blue teapot below is the one normally found on this shape teapot produced for the Gold Decorated Line. These teapots will be found in sizes ranging from one cup to eight cups. Also, notice the sugar and creamer of the same shape with a matching decoration.

The pink teapot is from the Gold Label Line. These teapots are decorated with an all-over fleur-de-lis pattern and have golden handles, spouts and knobs. The usual color found with this decoration is Dresden, but other colors will also be found.

Baltimore

Prices of standard gold decorated teapots are about the same as the same color undecorated teapots.

Common and less collectible colors: Most greens, most lighter blues, yellows, black, maroon, pink and ivory.

Unusual and more collectible colors: Rose, orchid, red and cobalt.

Teapot	Common Color	Unusual Color	Gold Label	Decal Decoration
Baltimore	18.00-20.00	35.00-45.00	40.00-45.00	30.00-40.00

Row 1: Baltimore, maroon Gold Label; Baltimore, ivory with pink rose decal; Baltimore, cadet/standard gold. **Row 2:** Boston, pink with Gold Label Fleur-de-lis; Boston, Dresden/standard gold sugar and creamer with matching teapot.

Boston Teapots

The rose teapot and the black teapots are examples of early gold decorations. The design on the rose teapot is referred to as "Trailing Astor." The black teapot utilizes the same gold floral decoration which is normally found on the French-shape teapots. This design is usually called "French Flower." Notice the handle and spout of this teapot are gold encrusted.

The silver teapot is from a short-lived Hall experiment to develop a chip-proof teapot. This regular china teapot has been coated with a nickel alloy by an outside company. Production during the 1950's was limited as attempts to perfect this idea were unsuccessful. Several other shapes of metal-clad teapots and coffee pots will also be found.

The gold coated set is from Hall's Golden Glo line. The bright gold glaze has been applied over a Hi-white base. The Golden Glo line is quite extensive and many of these pieces were made as early as the 1940's. However, some pieces are still in production. For more information about the items available in this line, see the Golden Glo listing under kitchenware.

The Boston shape has been subjected to various decal applications. Hall developed a retail teapot line during the 1960's in which a Boston teapot with a decal was used. The body of this teapot was green and it contained a golden fruit decal in a band around the center. This shape teapot has also been used in some of the regular decal dinnerware and kitchenware lines.

Prices of teapots with the standard gold decoration are about the same as undecorated teapots of the same color.

Common and less collectible colors: all greens, all browns, most lighter blues, yellows, black, maroon, pink, ivory and grey.

Unusual and more collectible colors: Red, cobalt, rose, orchid and turquoise.

Row 1: Boston, rose color with gold Trailing Astor design; Boston, black with gold French Flower decoration; Boston, Hi-white. **Row 2:** Boston, metal-clad; Boston, Golden Glo sugar, creamer and matching teapot.

Teapot	Common Color	Unusual Color	Early Gold Design	Gold Label
Boston, 1-, 1½-, 2-cup	20.00-25.00	27.00-32.00	35.00-40.00	25.00-30.00
Boston, 3-, 4-cup	15.00-20.00	25.00-30.00	27.00-32.00	25.00-30.00
Boston, 6-cup	15.00-18.00	27.00-32.00	35.00-40.00	25.00-30.00
Boston, 8-cup	15.00-20.00	27.00-32.00	35.00-45.00	28.00-32.00

Cleveland Teapots

The Cleveland is a six-cup teapot which was introduced in the late 1930's. It is most commonly found in emerald with gold decoration, but is also available in other colors with and without gold decoration. The standard gold decoration is shown on the two gold decorated teapots in the picture. Those collectors who are seeking undecorated teapots will have to be more patient than those looking for gold decorated ones. However, prices for both types are currently about the same for equivalant colors.

Common and less collectible colors: turquoise, all yellows, all greens.

Unusual and more collectible colors: Most blues, red, grey, orchid, rose and maroon.

Left to right: Cleveland, turquoise; Cleveland, warm yellow with standard gold; Cleveland, emerald with standard gold.

Teapot	Common Colors	Unusual Colors
Cleveland	30.00-32.00	35.00-45.00

Hollywood Teapots

The Hollywood teapot first appeared in the late 1920's. It may be found in the three sizes illustrated here–4-cup, 6-cup and 8-cup. There is also a matching sugar and creamer available for some decorations. The standard decoration is shown on the two teapots at each end of the top row. The black teapot in the center is an example of the Gold Label decoration. A more commonly found color with this decoration is pink.

The pearlized-color teapot shown on the second row is uncommon. The "special" gold treatment of the handle and spout add to the appeal of this teapot. Several other shapes of teapots with this unusual color glaze have been found. These are highly desirable additions to the collections of teapot lovers.

The Hollywood teapot is often found in maroon and in a variety of greens and the lighter blue colors. Also, the six-cup size is the most common of the three sizes.

Common or less collectible colors: all greens, all browns, black, maroon, all lighter blues, all yellows, pink and ivory.

Unusual or more collectible colors: red, cobalt, rose, orchid, grey and Dresden.

The standard gold decorated teapots will be priced about the same as undecorated teapots of the same color.

Row 1: Hollywood, 8-cup stock green/gold; Hollywood, 6-cup Hi-black/Gold Label; Hollywood, 4-cup emerald/gold. **Row 2:** Hollywood, pearl-color/"special" gold; Hollywood-shape creamer and sugar.

Teapot	Common Colors	Unusual Colors*	Gold Label
Hollywood, 4-cup	27.00-30.00	35.00-45.00	
Hollywood, 6-cup	15.00-20.00	35.00-45.00	35.00-40.00
Hollywood, 8-cup	15.00-24.00	35.00-45.00	
Sugar/Creamer	12.00-14.00	18.00-20.00	

* Pearl-color glaze, 60.00-70.00.

Illinois, Los Angeles and Newport Teapots

The Illinois is a very hard-to-find six-cup teapot which dates to the 1930's. The standard gold decoration is pictured, and we are aware of another gold decoration for this teapot. This decoration consists of gold spirals which form a series of circles near the top of the teapot. The colors which are found most readily appear to be cobalt and maroon.

The Los Angeles teapot may be found in three sizes – eight-cup, six-cup and four-cup. Of the three sizes, the six cup is the most common. This teapot first appeared in the mid-1920's and was subjected to a number of different decorations during its many years of production. The standard gold decoration may be seen on the emerald four-cup teapot to the right and the Gold Label version is illustrated by the pink teapot in the center. In addition to gold decoration, decals were also applied to this shape teapot. A 1930's floral band decal is shown circling the upper body on the eight-cup teapot pictured on the left side of the bottom row. A band of green leaves is often found in this same position on a mustard color teapot which was produced during the 1960's.

The Newport teapot was introduced in the 1930's. It will be found in both seven-cup and five-cup sizes. This teapot was used in the Autumn Leaf pattern and is most commonly found with that decal in the seven-cup size. In addition, the Newport will be found in a variety of solid colors and with gold and decal decorations. The standard gold decoration consists of a narrow gold floral band near the top of the teapot and a matching floral band on the lid. The handle and spout are also trimmed with gold lines. A decal decoration for the Newport is pictured. This decoration is from the 1930's and features a bouquet of multi-colored flowers in black urn. The handle, spout and lid are also accented with black trim.

Illinois common colors: maroon, canary and cobalt.

Illinois unusual colors: any other colors.

Los Angeles common colors: all greens, pink, cobalt, maroon and brown.

Los Angeles unusual colors: red, most blues, orchid and rose.

Newport common colors: pink, stock green, stock brown and ivory.

Newport unusual colors: all other colors.

Teapot	Common Colors	Unusual Colors	Decal Decorated	Gold Label
Illinois	75.00-95.00	100.00-125.00		
Los Angeles, 8-cup	22.00-27.00	35.00-45.00	45.00-55.00	
Los Angeles, 6-cup	18.00-22.00	35.00-40.00	45.00-55.00	35.00-40.00
Los Angeles, 4-cup	22.00-27.00	40.00-45.00		
Newport*	18.00-22.00	35.00-45.00	40.00-50.00	

* Gold decorated, add 20%.

Row 1: Illinois, maroon/standard gold; Illinois, stock brown/standard gold; Newport, pink/flower pot decal. **Row 2:** Los Angeles, 8-cup with milky blue glaze and flower band decoration; Los Angeles, 6-cup pink/Gold Label; Los Angeles, 4-cup emerald/standard gold.

New York Teapots

The New York teapot was added to the Gold decorated line from the institutional line in 1920. In the ensuing years, it was to become one of the most successful of all Hall teapots. It will be found in more colors, sizes and decorations than any other Hall teapot. The New York shape was also used in many of the decal lines and was the teapot shape selected by the National Autumn Leaf Collectors Club for their first limited edition piece produced by Hall. The New York teapot is still being produced for the institutional line. To identify the newer teapots, look for the square Hall backstamp.

Nine different sizes – 1-, 1½-, 2-, 3-, 4-, 6-, 8-, 10-, 12-cup – of the New York teapot have been produced. Today collectors are finding the four-, six- and eight-cup sizes most often. The other larger and smaller sizes appear less frequently. The standard gold decoration is best seen on the Dresden teapot with the matching sugar and creamer.

The older New York teapots are appearing primarily in the cobalt color. These teapots are generally identified by their non-standard gold decorations and their early backstamp. The early backstamp used on the teapots during the 1920's is like the #2 backstamp shown in the identification section or may be a slight variation. In the variations, the "Made in U.S.A." is missing or is outside the circle.

The green teapot on the right side of the top row is referred to as a "special." It has the standard gold decoration along with a gold encrusted handle and spout. The teapot shown on the left side of the top row is very unusual. The decoration consists of an all-over floral pattern and extensive gold embellishment. Handpainted gold and enamel decorations also consist of a palm leaf design similar to the one seen on the French teapot (shown on page 183) and the Burbick design pictured on the left side of the third row. Three different combinations of game bird decals consisting of ducks, pheasants or grouse have been found by collectors. These decals are usually found on four-cup and six-cup teapots, but are also known to exist in the two-cup size. The silver teapot shown on the right side of the third row is an example of a metal clad teapot. These teapots were coated with a special metal alloy to resist chipping.

The teapots in the bottom photograph represent various sizes and colors of the New York teapot with the Gold Label decoration.

In addition, the New York shape has been found with the same multi-colored floral and black urn decal which is pictured on the Newport teapot shown on page 195. This decal dates to the 1930's and is not commonly found today.

Common or less collectible colors: lighter blues, all greens, all browns, all yellows, ivory, pink and black.

Unusual or more collectible colors: red, cobalt, blue turquoise, rose and orchid.

The standard gold decorated teapots are priced the same as the undecorated teapots of the same color.

Teapot	Common Colors	Unusual Colors	Old Gold Decoration	Gold Label	Decal Decorated
New York, 1-2 cup	18.00-20.00	27.00-32.00	35.00-37.00	27.00-32.00	55.00-65.00
New York, 3-4 cup	16.00-18.00	27.00-32.00	35.00-40.00	27.00-32.00	55.00-65.00
New York, 6-8 cup	12.00-14.00	27.00-30.00	35.00-40.00	27.00-30.00	50.00-60.00
New York, 10-12 cup	22.00-25.00	30.00-35.00	40.00-45.00	27.00-32.00	
New York sugar and creamer	9.00-12.00	14.00-18.00			

Row 1: New York, paisley decoration/gold; New York, canary/gold band; New York, stock green/gold "special." **Row 2:** New York, Dresden/standard gold with matching sugar and creamer; New York, stock green/standard gold. **Row 3:** New York, cobalt with enameled "Burbick" decoration; New York, game bird decal; New York, metal clad.

New York Teapots with Gold Label Decoration.

Row 1: New York, 12-cup blue turquoise; New York, 10-cup black; New York, 8-cup pink. **Row 2:** New York, 6-cup matte pink; New York, 4-cup ivory; New York, 2-cup cadet.

Teapot Miscellany

The Bowling Ball, a teapot from the late 1930's, was very successful at disguising its existence until a few years ago. After its initial confirmation as a Hall teapot, a virtual avalanche of Bowling Balls appeared. Recently, it seems as if this teapot has gone back into hiding again and really may be as scarce as was once thought. The usual color it is found in is turquoise. We have seen one in cobalt and have not heard of the Bowling Ball being found in any other color or with any gold decoration.

The "Philbe" is illustrated by the canary teapot on the top row. This is only the second one of this shape teapots we have seen. The other one was cobalt with a "special" style gold decoration and was pictured in the first book. The original source for this teapot could confirm this is a Hall teapot, but could not contribute any other details on its history.

The Tip-Pot was made by Hall for the Forman Family. It has two spouts, but only one internal chamber and is designed to fit into the candle warmer style holder shown in the picture. The Tip-Pot backstamp reads: "TIP-POT–The ultimate in serving hot tea or coffee. 10 cup–FIREPROOF–HALL CHINA–ANOTHER FORMAN FAMILY PRODUCT." For more information on Forman Family products see the coffee pot section.

The round T-Ball was introduced in 1948. It was made by Hall for Bacharach of New York and has the following backstamp: "T-BALL TEAPOT–MADE FOR BACHARACH BY HALL CHINA COMPANY." A number of undecorated colors may be found and a black teapot with gold decoration also exists. The black one does not have the Bacharach backstamp. Instead it has a "HALL" mark and gold number (0850GL), with the letters "GL" possibly indicating this teapot was a part of the Gold Label line.

The square T-Ball was also made for Bacharach in the late 1940's. This teapot is currently being produced as part of the Hall American line. The old teapots will have the Bacharach backstamp. Both the round and square versions of the T-Ball have a side pocket on each side in which a teabag may be placed.

The "Rutherford" teapot is the same shape as the "Ribbed" teapot shown in the kitchenware section. This smooth version is shown here with green trim. It will also be found with decals in some of the dinnerware lines and in the Buffet Service in matte white decorated with dots.

The cobalt Ohio teapot with the gold decoration in the center of the third row is one of the older gold decorated teapots. This teapot is usually found in pink or black with a gold dot decoration.

The Kansas and Indiana are two teapots which are still lacking from many collections. Both will be found with gold decoration more often than without. The usual gold decorations and most common colors may be seen in the photograph.

The French drip coffee biggin is actually a coffee pot with its dripper in place. However, it can also be used as a teapot with the dripper removed. It may be found in numerous colors and in sizes ranging from two-cup to eight-cup. We have not seen it with gold decoration. Common colors are stock brown, stock green and canary.

Teapot	Common Color	Unusual Color
Bowling Ball	200.00-250.00	
French drip coffee biggin	30.00-35.00	40.00-50.00
Indiana	95.00-110.00	110.00-135.00
Kansas	95.00-110.00	120.00-155.00
Ohio	85.00-95.00	120.00-150.00
"Philbe"	UND	UND
"Rutherford"	45.00-55.00	60.00-70.00
T-Ball round	35.00-45.00	55.00-65.00
T-Ball square	30.00-40.00	45.00-50.00
Tip-Pot	50.00-55.00	75.00-85.00

Row 1: Bowling Ball, turquoise; "Philbe," canary; Tip-Pot, ivory. **Row 2:** T-Ball, round, black/gold; T-Ball, round, emerald; T-Ball, square, cobalt. **Row 3:** "Rutherford, with green trim; Ohio, cobalt/gold; Kansas, emerald/gold. **Row 4:** Indiana, warm yellow/gold; French drip coffee biggin, canary; French drip coffee biggin, blue.

Victorian Style Teapots

Six Victorian style six-cup teapots were introduced in the early 1940's. This was not a dramatically successful line and gold decoration was later added to help stimulate sales. However, success was not attained and the line was dropped by the end of the decade. As a result, undecorated teapots are available in sufficient quantity, but collectors are having great difficulty obtaining decorated teapots.

An ad from a 1947 catalog illustrates that two of these teapots–the "Plume" and "Murphy"–were sold by Jewel for $1.75 each.

For the most part, each teapot is only available in a single color. However, an occasional one may be found in an odd color. An example is the "Benjamin," which has been found in a gold color as well as the usual green.

The amount of gold decoration varies considerably among the different shapes. The "Benjamin," "Birch," and "Connie" feature generous gold decoration. They each have gold encrusted handles, and spouts along with liberal gold use on the teapot body. The "Plume," "Murphy," and "Bowknot," display a conservative use of gold.

Teapot	Common Color	Unusual Color	Gold Decorated
"Benjamin"	20.00-22.00	30.00-40.00	55.00-65.00
"Birch"	18.00-20.00		60.00-70.00
"Bowknot"	25.00-27.00	30.00-40.00	40.00-45.00
"Connie"	18.00-20.00		55.00-60.00
"Murphy"	22.00-25.00		40.00-45.00
"Plume"	16.00-18.00		35.00-40.00

HALL TEA POTS

5H118   each, **$1.75**

Genuine Hall Teapots in charming pastel shades. Two styles from which to choose: one in pink (left) and one in blue (right). Their beauty is matched by their utility for they are made of glazed oven- ware that keeps sweet and clean. 6 cup size.

Order next time Your Friendly Jewel Man calls.

Hall China

Row 1: "Murphy," blue; "Benjamin," gold; "Bowknot," pink. **Row 2:** "Plume," pink; "Birch," blue/gold; "Connie," green.

Left to right: "Benjamin," green/gold; "Plume," pink/gold.

Thorley Teapots

A series of six new teapots which collectors call "Thorley Teapots" was introduced in the early 1950's. These teapots were designed by the noted J. Palin Thorley and were probably intended to replace the Victorian series teapots which had been discontinued due to lackluster sales. These teapots are officially known as the "Brilliant Series Group 120 Teapots."

Although the Thorley teapots are sometimes found plain, they are most often found with gaudy gold decoration. Some have glass rhinestones imbedded in small pockets formed in the body. Collectors are most interested in the teapots with rhinestones. This line, like the earlier Victorian series, was not highly successful, but these teapots still remained in the catalog as late as 1968. At that time the wholesale cost was $4.95 each.

As may be seen in the photograph, the Grape design teapot was also made with the Classic-shape Bouquet decal. In addition, several pieces of kitchenware were produced in the matching grape pattern. These include a set of three mixing bowls, a round, handled casserole and a cookie jar. These are usually found in yellow.

Teapot	Common Color	Gold Decorated	Rhinestone Decorated
"Apple"	55.00-60.00	65.00-75.00	
"Grape"	30.00-35.00	45.00-50.00	45.00-55.00
"Regal"	40.00-45.00	55.00-60.00	60.00-65.00
"Royal"	35.00-40.00	45.00-50.00	55.00-60.00
"Starlight"	27.00-30.00	32.00-37.00	45.00-55.00
"Windcrest"	25.00-30.00	30.00-35.00	35.00-40.00

Kitchenware	
Bowl, 6″	5.00-6.00
Bowl, 7½″	6.00.700
Bowl, 8¾″	8.00-9.00
Casserole	16.00-18.00
Cookie jar	20.00-22.00

Ad from 1968 Bostwick-Brown Company catalogue

Left to right: Cookie jar, "Grape"; casserole, "Grape"; teapot, "Grape" with gold band.

Row 1: "Grape," ivory with blue rhinestones; "Grape," yellow with gold band; "Grape," ivory with Bouquet decal. **Row 2:** "Regal," maroon; "Regal," apple green/gold; "Starlight," lemon. **Row 3:** "Windcrest," lemon/gold; "Apple," sky blue/gold; "Royal," ivory.

Pert and E-Style Teapots

"Pert" teapots are a part of the kitchenware line. This shape teapot is more commonly associated with some of the decal lines, but gold decorated teapots in this shape also exist. They are usually found in cadet or yellow with gold decoration on the handle, spout and around the lid opening. The undecorated teapot found most often has a Chinese red body with a Hi-white handle.

E-style teapots, a familiar shape to collectors of Cameo Rose, are showing up decorated with other decals and with gold. Two are pictured below. Other decal decorations also have been found. Although these decorated teapots are not common, there has not been much collector interest in this shape teapot.

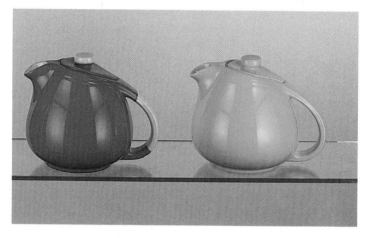

"Pert," Chinese red and Hi-white; "Pert," canary/gold.

Teapot	Chinese Red	Common Colors	Gold Decorated
"Pert," 3-cup	16.00-18.00	16.00-18.00	25.00-30.00
"Pert," 6-cup	18.00-22.00	18.00-22.00	25.00-30.00
E-style			25.00-32.00

E-style teapots, gold decorated and floral decorated.

No. 1 Tea Set and No. 2 Coffee Set

The No. 1 Tea Set and No. 2 Coffee Set were both introduced in the early 1950's. Both the coffee set and tea set came in two colors and with three different floral decorations. The yellow color is called Buttercup and the light blue color is Blue Belle. The three decorations are 80-B, a blue flower, 80-Y, a yellow flower and 80-P, a pink flower. Both sets are trimmed with gold lines.

The Tea Set uses the Morning Set teapot and creamer shapes. However, the similarity between the two sets ends there. The shape of the sugar is different and a cup and party plate have been added. The Morning Set sugar has handles and a lid. The No. 1 Tea Set sugar is open and has no handles. Also the Morning Set does not have cups and saucers. The party plates have an off-center ring upon which the teacup fits. The party plates to the Tea Set are round while the plates to the Coffee Set are scalloped.

The No. 2 Coffee Set has an open sugar with a ruffled top and a tall creamer with a handle and general shape that matches the coffee pot. This coffee pot shape is also used in the Golden Glo line and a larger version, which bears the Drip-O-lator backstamp, may be found decorated with a floral decal.

Row 1: No. 1 Tea Set in Blue Belle color: open sugar; 21 oz. teapot; cream pitcher; tea cup and party plate. **Row 2:** No. 2 Coffee Set in Buttercup color: open sugar; 24 oz. coffee pot; cream pitcher; coffee cup; party plate.

	Coffee Set	**Tea Set**
Coffee pot	45.00-50.00	
Creamer	10.00-12.00	9.00-11.00
Cup	9.00-10.00	9.00-10.00
Plate	6.00-8.00	6.00-8.00
Sugar	10.00-12.00	9.00-11.00
Teapot		45.00-50.00

Early Gold Decorated and Art Deco Teapots

The teapots in the two photos in the center of this page are from an early gold decorated line which probably dates to the mid-1920's. The three teapots shown here and the cobalt and gold Ohio shown on page 201 are teapots we believe were a part of this early series. Other similar teapots may show up, but they are uncommon enough at this time to prevent lending any insight into their history.

The 10-sided cobalt "Columbia" teapot shown in the center photo has the #2 backstamp with the numbers 15-80 in place of the usual "MADE IN U.S.A." We have only seen one other teapot like this and it was also cobalt with the same gold decoration.

The "Johnson" teapot is an elegantly designed piece with liberal gold decoration. The long spout and gently rounded handle add grace and balance to the finished teapot.

The "Naomi" teapot has six panelled sides. Each panel has a gold decorated emblem and is outlined with a gold border.

The teapots shown in the bottom photo are from what appears to be a three teapot series which collectors are calling "Deco." Researchers have assigned the names "Adele," "Damascus," and "Danielle" to these three teapots. The colors which are being found most often are olive green, light blue, maroon and yellow. Each one turns up most often in one basic color, but all have been found in more than one of the above colors.

"Johnson," cobalt/gold; Naomi, cobalt/gold.

"Columbia," cobalt/gold.

Item	Common Colors	Gold Decorated
"Adele"	45.00-55.00	
"Damascus"	50.00-55.00	
"Danielle"	50.00-55.00	
"Columbia"		175.00-195.00
"Johnson"		150.00-175.00
"Naomi"		110.00--120.00

Left to right: "Adele"; "Damascus"; "Danielle."

Musical Teapots

Hall produced a six-cup musical teapot in the mid-1950's. The teapot was advertised for $6.95 in a 1954 Montgomery Ward Christmas catalog. It has been found most often in the blue color shown in the picture below, but other colors may be found as well. The teapot has a cavity on the under side into which the wind-up music box fits. Appropriately, the music box plays "Tea For Two." Numerous teapots are being found with their music boxes missing.

Left to right: Musical teapot, blue; musical teapot, ivory with maroon and gold trim.

Teapot	Price
Musical teapot	70.00-90.00*

* Priced with working music box.

Twin-Tee and Tea-For-Two Teapots

The Twin-Tee sets consist of a hot water pot (short spout) and a pot for holding the brewed tea (long spout). There is also a matching divided tray which serves as a trivet for the hot pots. The Twin-Tee sets were introduced in 1926 and may be found in numerous colors. Collectors like these small sets because of the different decals and interesting gold decorations which have been applied to them.

Tea for Two sets also are comprised of two pots and a matching tray. However, these sets differ from the Twin-Tee sets in several ways. The tops of the Tea for Two pots are angled rather than straight and the trays do not have the full-length center division like the Twin-Tee trays. There is also a larger version of this set called Tea for Four.

Row 1: Twin-Tee, Black Garden design; Twin-Tee, Pansy decal; Twin-Tee, rose/gold. **Row 2:** Twin-Tee, stock green/gold; Twin-Tee, cobalt; Twin-Tee, daffodil with black trim.

Tea for Two, pink/platinum decoration.

Teapot	Common Colors	Unusual Colors	Gold/Decal Decoration
Tea for Two	30.00-35.00	40.00-45.00	65.00-75.00
Tea for Four	40.00-45.00	55.00-60.00	65.00-80.00
Twin-Tee	30.00-35.00	40.00-50.00	55.00-65.00

Cube and Dohrmann Teapots

Cubes are two-cup teapots made by Hall and several other companies under a British patent. The Hall teapots will have the Hall #3 backstamp, the patent numbers and the following inscription on the bottom: "CUBE TEAPOTS, LIMITED, LEICESTER." Although the Cube-shape teapots have been found in numerous colors, very few have been found with gold decoration.

Hall produced the teapot shown at the bottom of this page for the Dohrmann Company. This company operated in the Western states and most of the teapots will be found in that geographical area. The teapots have the following backstamp: "DORHCO" and the HALL mark in a circle with "MADE IN U.S.A." underneath.

Left: Cube, emerald. **Right:** Cube, black.

Cube, blue/gold.

Dohrco teapot.

Teapot	Red/Cobalt	Other Colors	Gold Decorated
Cube	40.00-45.00	32.00-37.00	60.00-65.00
Dohrco		20.00-25.00	

Coverlet and McCormick Teapots

The "Coverlet" teapot has a metal cover with cut-outs for the handle and spout. The teapot in the center has the metal cover removed to show the shape of the teapot. These teapots are marked "Made exclusively for the FORMAN FAMILY, INC. by THE HALL CHINA CO., U.S.A." The teapot may be found in various colors and came with either a silver or gold color cover. A matching sugar and creamer set are shown in the photo below.

The McCormick teapot was made as a premium item for the McCormick Tea Company. The teapots are marked "McCORMICK, BALTIMORE, MARYLAND." The most commonly found colors are maroon, turquoise, light blue and stock brown. McCormicks have been found with gold decoration and in the two-cup size with a large raised "Mc" on the side. A few older McCormick teapots have a lid which locks into the infusor. In this teapot, the lid completely conceals the infusor when it is in place, and both the lid and infusor are removed from the teapot as one piece. The body of these teapots differs slightly from a normal McCormick. There is a built-in strainer at the tip of the spout and the lid has a loop handle rather than a knob.

Row 1: "Coverlet," canary; "Coverlet," pink; "Coverlet," ivory. **Row 2:** McCormick, turquoise; McCormick, maroon; McCormick, light blue.

"Coverlet" sugar and creamer.

Teapot	Common Colors	Gold Decorated
"Coverlet"	18.00-20.00	
McCormick, 6-cup	15.00-20.00	30.00-35.00
McCormick, 2-cup	16.00-18.00	

Teamaster Teapots

Different shapes of teapots which Hall produced for the Teamaster Company are shown in the photographs on this page.

The Teataster is an oval, two-compartment teapot which was made for Teamaster in the 1940's. Most of the teapots are plain, but a few will be found with gold decoration. The backstamp states: "TEAMASTER, MADE BY HALL IN U.S.A."

Twinspouts are round 2-compartment teapots produced for the Teamaster Company. The teapots are usually marked "TWINSPOUT, TEAMASTER, Pat. No. 2135410." Twinspouts will be found with gold decoration and some have been found with sterling silver overlay. Later teapots made in this shape will be marked "INVENTO PRODUCTS."

The three-cup diamond-shape Twinspout teapots below are also two-compartment teapots. They were made for Teamaster and have the same backstamp as the Twinspouts above. We have not seen this teapot decorated.

Left to right: Teataster, turquoise; Twinspout, emerald; Twinspout, warm yellow; Twinspout, canary/gold.

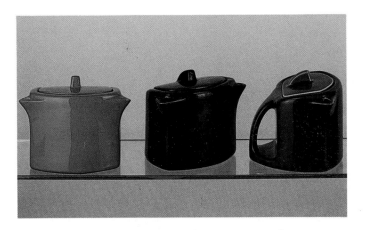

Left to right: Alma, Chinese red; Alma, turquoise; Alma, maroon.

Teapot	Undecorated	Gold Decorated
Alma, 3-cup	40.00-47.00	
Teataster	50.00-55.00	50.00-60.00
Twinspout	40.00-45.00	45.00-50.00

Coffee Pots

The Washington coffee pot was introduced in 1919. The retail price of a nine-cup Washington was $1.89 in a Montgomery Ward catalog from that year. This coffee pot is still being made, and it has appeared in many different colors and with numerous styles of decoration over the long span of production. Sizes in which the Washington coffee pot has been produced include: 1-, 1½-, 2-, 6-, 12- and 15-cup.

Researchers have christened the large red and white teapot on the second row "Deca-flip." It is usually found in this color combination, but may on occasion be found with the color pattern reversed.

The "Baron" is seen most often in Chinese red, but may also be found in other colors. It is not an easy coffee pot to find.

The green "Alcony" coffee pot almost appears to be a large version of the short-spout "Carraway" which was made for Tricolator. The lid and handle on the two coffee pots appear to be identical in design. The coffee pot below has the #3 backstamp.

Row 1: Washington, stock brown with gold French Flower design; Washington, cobalt with early gold design; Washington, Hi-white with orange "Dutch" decal. **Row 2:** "Deca-flip," Red/Hi-white; "Baron," Chinese red; "Alcony" green.

Coffee Pot	Common Color	Gold Decorated	Coffee Pot	Common Color	Gold Decorated
"Alcony"	20.00-22.00		Washington, 1- to 2-cup	9.00-12.00	18.00-22.00
"Baron"	32.00-35.00		Washington, 6-cup	12.00-15.00	20.00-25.00
"Deca-flip"	28.00-32.00		Washington, 12- & 15-cup	18.00-22.00	35.00-45.00

Drip Coffee Pot Shapes

A number of different shapes of all-china drip coffee pots were produced by Hall. The complete coffee pot is comprised of four pieces. There is the base, a china dripper, a china spreader which fits inside the dripper and a lid. Most of these shapes were used in the decal lines. Some of the more common shapes are pictured here to help with identification and for ease of comparison. A shape which is not shown here is "Medallion." This shape may be seen on page 119.

The #691 coffee pot is usually found in solid colors or decorated as shown below. The colors may vary, as we have seen red, blue and green bands. Flamingo is the only decal we have seen on this shape, although there may be others.

The middle coffee pot on the top row is unusual in that it has an electric warmer base made of metal. The design on the one in the picture is the only one we have seen on this shape.

The Jordan drip coffee pot is most commonly associated with the Autumn Leaf pattern. However, this shape drip coffee pot is also found in a number of other decal patterns. It is not common, but it has also been seen in cadet with a Hi-white handle and lid. The distinguishing feature of this coffee pot is its vertical panels which are separated by distinct vertical ribs.

The "Kadota" coffee pot has a smooth body. We have only seen this in ivory in various decal patterns. Usually the backstamp is the Drip-O-lator mark.

The distinctive feature of the "Radiance" coffee pot is the series of rays which separate the body into vertical panels. This coffee pot may be found in solid colors and is used with decal applications over an ivory body.

The E-style coffee pot has only been found in a single pattern—Mount Vernon. This pattern was designed by J. Palin Thorley and was sold by Sears during the 1950's.

Prices are only for the colors and decorations indicated. The decal pattern coffee pots are priced with their respective patterns.

Row 1: #691 drip coffee, ivory with blue band and platinum trim; metal base drip coffee; Jordan drip coffee, Crocus pattern. **Row 2:** "Kadota" drip coffee, Shaggy Tulip decal; "Radiance" drip coffee, #488 decal; E-style drip coffee, Mount Vernon pattern.

Coffee Pot	Price
#691, solid color	45.00-55.00
#691, color band	55.00-65.00
Metal base, as pictured	55.00-60.00
E-style Mt. Vernon	60.00-70.00

Coffee Pot	Price
Jordan, cadet/Hi-white	42.00-47.00
"Radiance," solid colors*	65.00-70.00

* Red/cobalt, 95.00-110.00.

Drip-O-lator Coffee Pots

Hall made coffee pot bodies for the Enterprise Aluminum Company of Massillon, Ohio. Enterprise supplied the aluminum dripper for these coffee pots and marketed the finished product. Some shapes will be found in more than one size. Although many shapes appear to be limited to a single decoration, there are a few coffee pot styles which will be found with numerous decorations. Other companies besides Hall also supplied china bases to the Enterprise Company. In some cases these bodies will bear the backstamp of the manufacturer, but the coffee pots produced by Hall will only have the Drip-O-lator mark. The coffee pot shapes known to be made by Hall will be illustrated and priced on the following pages. All the names of both the shapes and decorations have been contributed by researchers.

Opposite Page: The "Trellis is pictured in a solid color. It may also be found with a V-shaped, multi-colored floral decoration. The "Bauhaus" is usually found with the two floral decorations pictured. The "Waverly" is shown with the Yellow Rose decal here. On page 218, it is also pictured with the Minuet decal and with an irridized gold fleurette design. This coffee pot may be found with both styles of lids that are pictured and is available in two sizes. The "Cathedral" coffee pot is available in two sizes and the same daisy-like decal is also found on a few kitchenware pieces. See the miscellaneous page in the kitchenware section. Ths "Sash" is also found with a blue band with white stars. This coffee pot is known as the "Orb" with the colored, molded band smoothed over and replaced with a decal. The "Meltdown" is a shape which is very similar to a Drip-O-lator coffee pot produced by Fraunfelter. The biggest difference between the two is a slightly longer spout on the Hall coffee pot.

Drip-O-lator	Price	Drip-O-lator	Price
Bauhaus	28.88-32.00	Orb	22.00-27.00
Bricks and Ivy	25.00-30.00	Panel	20.00-25.00
Cathedral	18.00-22.00	Petal	27.00-32.00
Coffee Set shape	35.00-40.00	Rounded Terrace	16.00-20.00
Dart	22.00-27.00	Sash	20.00-25.00
Drape	18.00-22.00	Scoop	30.00-35.00
Duse	22.00-27.00	Target	25.00-30.00
Jerry	25.00-30.00	Trellis	25.00-30.00
Kadota all-china	45.00-55.00	Viking	18.00-22.00
Lotus	30.00-35.00	Waverly	18.00-22.00
Meltdown	27.00-32.00	Wicker	28.00-32.00

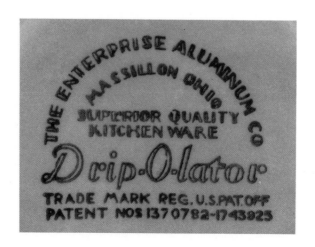

Row 1: "Trellis"; "Bauhaus," Jonquil decal; "Bauhaus," Juneflower decal. **Row 2:** "Waverly," Yellow Rose decal; "Drape," mini-floral decal; "Jerry." **Row 3:** "Cathedral," "Sash"; "Viking," Cactus decal. **Row 4:** "Petal," large-size, "Petal," small-size; "Meltdown."

Row 1: "Waverly," small-size with dome lid and Minuet decal; "Waverly," large-size with Minuet decal; "Waverly," irridized gold mini-fleurette design. **Row 2:** "Bricks and Ivy"; "Wicker"; "Rounded Terrace," Pasture Rose decal.

Left to Right: "Rounded Terrace," Bouquet decal; "Target"; "Scoop," Wildflower decal.

Left to right: "Kadota" all-china drip with Morning Flower decal; "Kadota" all-china drip with Wildflower decal; "Dart," pink rose decal.

Numerous "Kadota" shape all-china drip coffee pots will be found with the Drip-O-lator backstamp. However, not all of the coffee pots of this shape were made for Enterprise. Matching covered sugars and creamers may be found for both the "Dart" and "Duse shapes.

Row 1: "Panel," potted flower decal; "Lotus," Impatiens decal; Coffee Set shape. **Row 2:** "Duse" coffee pot; "Duse" creamer; "Dart" creamer.

Forman Family Products

Products with the Forman Family backstamp represent the end result of a joint effort between Hall and Forman to produce useful articles from a combination of china and chrome. Teapots, coffee pots, casseroles and electric percolators are the most common items which were finished by the Forman Family workers.

The "Dutch" teapot is very similar to the "Diver" teapot which Hall produced for Tricolator. The lid of the "Dutch fits over the top edge, while the lid of the "Diver" fits inside the top rim. The shape of the tips of the spouts also differs slightly.

The electric warmer holds three Petite Marmites and was designed to keep food warm. In another application, ice could also be packed around the marmites to chill food.

Row 1: "Edwards" teapot with blue-trimmed Mother of Pearl body; "Russell" coffee pot with Fuji decal; Fuji decal sugar and creamer. **Row 2:** "Dutch" teapot with Eden Bird decal; "Double Octagon" casserole with Eden Bird decal; "Ribbed Buffet" casserole with Pastel Floral decal.

Left: Electric warmer with three Petite Marmites. **Right:** Art Deco casserole in metal holder.

Item	Price	Item	Price
Casserole, Art Deco	25.00-30.00	Teapot, Dutch	30.00-35.00
Casserole, black/gold	20.00-25.00	Teapot, Edwards	37.00-42.00
Casserole, Double Octagon	20.00-25.00	Teapot, Tip-Pot	50.00-55.00
Casserole, Ribbed Buffet	16.00-20.00	Percolator, electric	50.00-70.00
Coffee pot, Russell	30.00-32.00	Waffle iron, Fuji	30.00-35.00
Creamer and sugar, Black/gold	12.00-15.00	Warmer, electric	37.00-40.00
Creamer and sugar, Fuji	18.00-20.00		

Row 1: Creamer, Straw Weave design, black/gold; electric percolator, Straw Weave design, black/gold; sugar, Straw Weave design, black/gold. **Row 2:** Casserole, black/gold; teapot, Tip-Pot, black/gold.

Tricolator Products

Hall produced numerous pots for Tricolator which may usually be identified through their backstamps. Many times "HALL" is embossed in the bottom in large block letters along with the words "Tricolator" or "Pour Right."

The coffee pot shape pictured below, which most collectors have been calling "Coffee Queen," actually has different names depending upon the size of the pot. According to the packing information enclosed with the coffee pots, the name of the four cup size is Princess; the six-cup size is Coffee Queen; the eight-cup is Empress. All sizes may be found in seven colors.

Most of the Tricolator coffee pots are being found in more than one color and some have been found with decals. The Carraway has also been found with a short spout. We have seen a picture of a long spout Carraway with enamel decoration.

The "Diver" has been found with several different decals. The shape of this teapot is very similar to the "Dutch" which Hall produced for Forman.

Coffee Pot	Price
Blossom	35.00-45.00
Buchanan	20.00-25.00
Carraway	18.00-22.00
Coffee Queen	12.00-14.00
Diver	30.00-35.00
Empress	14.00-16.00
Hoyt	20.00-25.00
Imperial	27.00-30.00
Princess	14.00-16.00
Ritz	30.00-35.00
Wellman	28.00-32.00

Coffee Queen with metal dripper.

Tricolator backstamp.

Row 1: "Blossom," green; "Blossom" irridescent tan with silver decal; "Hoyt," green. **Row 2:** "Ritz," red; "Wellman" blue. **Row 3:** "Diver," Floral Spray decal; "Carraway," long spout; "Imperial" green.

Tricolator Products

A panelled version of the "Wilson" has been found. It is called the "Amory." Notice the screw-lock lid of the "Buchanan." The pot has also been found without the locking lid. It will be found in other colors and with decals.

Row 1: "Lincoln," blue; "Lincoln," pink; "Wilson," brown. **Row 2:** "Ansel," red; "Buchanan," blue.

Coffee Pot	Price
Ansel	30.00-35.00
Buchanan	30.00-40.00
Wilson	20.00-25.00
Lincoln	30.00-37.00

Westinghouse

Westinghouse added the metal and electrical fixtures to the china percolator and coffee urn bodies produced by Hall. Two of the more successful patterns were Cattail and Hanging Vine. Today, the Cattail pattern is more desirable since it matches the popular Cattail dinnerware pattern produced by Universal.

Row 1: Coffee urn, Hanging Vine; sugar, Hanging Vine; electric percolator, Hanging Vine. **Row 2:** Electric percolator, Cattail; creamer and covered sugar, Cattail; coffee urn, Cattail.

Item	Price	Item	Price
Coffee urn, Cattail	65.00-75.00	Electric Percolator, Cattail	65.00-75.00
Coffee urn, Hanging Vine	35.00-45.00	Electric Percolator, Hanging Vine	30.00-40.00
Creamer, Cattail	12.00-15.00	Sugar and lid, Cattail	15.00-18.00
Creamer, Hanging Vine	6.00-8.00	Sugar and lid, Hanging Vine	8.00-10.00

Electric Percolators

The most commonly found shape of Hall electric percolator is the style used for the highly collectible percolator in the Autumn Leaf pattern. Today, this percolator with other decals is becoming more attractive to collectors.

Some of the numerous decals found on electric percolators will also be found on other accessory pieces. This has enabled collectors to put together matching mini sets of certain decals.

Some of the more popular decals found on the percolators are the series of game bird decals. Other accessory pieces found with the game bird decal are a casserole, a New York teapot, Windshield teapot and a "Thick Rim" bowl set.

In addition to the decals pictured, percolators with floral decals will be found. These decals appear less frequently than the game bird decals.

Another percolator with a gold Rx decoration is sometimes seen. The percolator is part of a set which was given as a premium to pharmacists. Other pieces available with this decoration include: a New York teapot, a cup and saucer, a casserole, an Irish coffee mug and a ¼# butter.

Game Bird Decal	Price
Bowl, 6″	8.00-10.00
Bowl, 7½″	10.00-12.00
Bowl, 8½″	12.00-15.00
Casserole	18.00-20.00
Percolator, electric	50.00-60.00
Teapot, New York	50.00-60.00
Teapot, Windshield	65.00-75.00

Rx Decoration	Price
Butter, ¼#	20.00-25.00
Casserole	10.00-15.00
Cup	4.00-5.00
Mug, Irish Coffee	5.00-7.00
Percolator, electric	20.00-25.00
Saucer	1.00-1.50
Teapot, New York	20.00-25.00

Other Percolators	Price
Floral decal	55.00-65.00
Gold deer	20.00-30.00
Solid color	30.00-32.00

Left to right: Electric percolator, geese decal; electric percolator, pink; electric percolator, pheasant decal.

Row 1: Electric percolator, gold deer decoration; electric percolator, Irish Setter decal. **Row 2:** Three piece "Thick Rim" game bird bowl set.

Part V: Other Hall Products

Beer Sets

Beer sets may be found in plain solid colors, with silver overlay or with decals. Basic sets consist of a tankard and six matching mugs. Decal sets will have three right-handed and three left-handed mugs. The tankard is pictured here with the flagon shape mug. Another style, the barrel shape mug is sometimes found with these sets.

The flagon is available in five sizes and the barrel mug comes in two sizes. Two different decals are shown–"Monk" and "Abbey Meal." Another decal depicting hunt scenes has been reported. A matching pretzel jar is also available for some decal sets.

	Solid Colors	Decals
Tankard pitcher	30.00-35.00	85.00-95.00
Flagon, 8, 10, 12, 14, 16 oz.	8.00-9.00	30.00-35.00
Barrel mug, 8, 12 oz.	7.00-9.00	
Pretzel jar	30.00-35.00	75.00-85.00

Old Crow Punch Set

The Old Crow punch set contains 10 cups, a ladle and a large elaborate advertising punch bowl. Initially these sets caused more excitement among collectors of advertising memorabilia than among Hall collectors. Some of the first sets were offered to collectors for as high as $450.

However, the quantity of available sets has proven substantial. Since the price of these sets has decreased and stabilized at a reasonable level, more Hall collectors have become attracted to them.

	Price
Set in original box	150.00-175.00
Bowl	80.00-90.00
Cup	4.00-6.00
Ladle	20.00-30.00

Tom and Jerry Sets

Tom and Jerry sets were introduced in the 1930's. They are commonly found with an ivory or Hi-black body and are usually trimmed with gold. The covered bowls hold five quarts and were sold with the #2044 mug.

	Price			Price
Covered Tom and Jerry bowl	30.00-35.00	Tom and Jerry #2044 mug		2.00-3.00

The Tom and Jerry bowl shown on the right holds four quarts and was sold with a five ounce mug. This style set has been found in at least one decal kitchenware line and also in the Eggshell Buffet Service line. The capacity of the Tom and Jerry Plum Pudding style bowl on the left is eight quarts. This bowl came with a seven ounce mug.

Item	Price	Item	Price
Tom and Jerry bowl, footed	20.00-25.00	Tom and Jerry mug, 5 oz.	1.75-2.25
Tom and Jerry Plum Pudding bowl	25.00-30.00	Tom and Jerry mug, 7 oz.	2.00-2.50

These four eight oz. pro-temperance mugs may have been produced for the Prohibition Party in 1934. All four mugs contain slogans denouncing the repeal of prohibition. The identity of two of the characters seems certain. One is Carry Nation, a noted temperance leader around the turn of the century. The mug with the caricature of Carry Nation asks the question, "Must I start all over again?" The figure with the beard is probably Congressman Andrew Volstead of Minnesota who was instrumental in engineering the passage of the National Prohibition Act. His comment is, "They surely crabbed my act." The other two figures are still unidentified, although they may have been prominent members of the Prohibition Party. The figure in blue assures, "It will still be grape juice for me," and the smiling character in red admonished, "I don't want it, you shouldn't have it."

Item	Price
Mug, 8 oz.	UND

The Hall watering can, which was produced in the early 1930's, is pictured here in all the colors we have seen. This early 1930's piece is very hard to find, and information is not extensive at this time, but red is the color most frequently found. The lavender color appears to be the least common.

Item	Price
Watering can	150.00-225.00

Promotional Products

Hall has produced many promotional pieces for private companies through the years. Since Hall China is primarily a hand operation, its facilities are easily adaptable to the special needs of individual customers.

Therefore, many items of this nature are still being made. Collectors should be aware the Sanka set and several other promotional pieces which were originally produced by Hall have recently been reproduced in Japan.

Row 1: Jug, "Teacher's Highland Cream"; jug, "Seagrams"; jug, "Vat 69." **Row 2:** Bowl, "Kraft Cheese"; Edgewater vase with hotel advertising; coffee pot, "Sanka"; mug, "Sanka."

Item	Price
Bowl, Kraft Cheese	6.00-8.00
Coffee pot, Sanka	8.00-10.00
Jug, Seagrams	5.00-7.00
Jug, Teacher's	8.00-10.00
Jug, Vat 69	6.00-8.00
Mug, Sanka	3.00-5.00
Vase, Edgewater	5.00-7.00

Vases, Mugs and Advertising Items

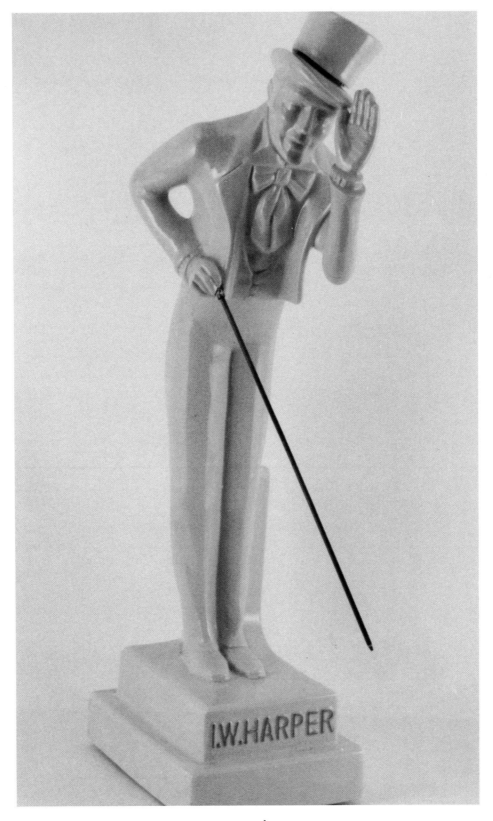

I.W. Harper decanter.

Hall produced a variety of items for hotels and restaurants. Some of these items are shown here.

		Price
Row 1:	1. This is not a Hall piece.	
	2. Trumpet vase, maroon	6.00-8.00
	3. Trumpet vase, cobalt	7.00-9.00
	4. Vase, daffodil	4.00-5.00
Row 2:	1. Turkish coffee cup, #1270	4.00-5.00
	2. Barrel mug, 8 oz.	5.00-6.00
	3. Mug, footed, #2274	4.00-5.00
	4. Braniff International mug	4.50-5.50
	5. Cylindrical mug, #1314	4.00-5.00
Row 3:	1. Ashtray, Palmer House	7.00-9.00
	2. Ashtray	6.00-8.00
	3. Ashtray	7.00-9.00
	4. Ashtray	6.00-8.00
	5. Ashtray with matchholder	5.00-7.00
Row 4:	1. Ashtray	6.00-7.00
	2. Ashtray	4.00-5.00
	3. Ashtray	6.00-8.00
	4. Ashtray, #696	3.00-4.00
Row 5:	1. Butter pat, Regency Hotel	2.50-3.50
	2. Ashtray, #679	3.00-4.00
	3. United Airlines bowl	7.00-9.00
	4. Spittoon	18.00-20.00
Previous page:	1. I.W. Harper decanter	40.00-50.00

Hall Lamps

A number of different Hall lamps have been showing up. Identification of the lamps is difficult unless the paper lable, which is usually in the shape of an Aladdin teapot, is still intact. Hall produced the china lamp bodies for other companies which added the metal bases and electrical fixtures.

Item	Price
Hall table lamp, solid color	27.00-32.00
Hall table lamp, handpainted	40.00-50.00
Hall table lamp, decal decoration	35.00-40.00

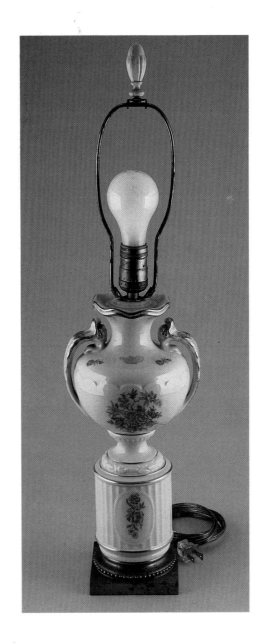

Nomenclature Cross Reference

Since Hall did not give names to every item produced, researchers have found it convenient to provide names to help with identification. In some cases more than one name has become associated with the same piece or shape. This listing will cross reference the multiple names for those collectors interested in using numerous references.

Names Used In This Reference	Other Names	Names Used In This Reference	Other Names
Adonis	Prince	Phoenix	Patrician
Apple	Browning	Plume	Disraeli
Baron	Big Boy	Radiance	Sunshine
Benjamen	Albert	Rayed	J-Sunshine
Birch	Darby	Regal	Dickens
Bowknot	Gladstone	Ribbed	Flute
Bowling Ball	Pepper	Rounded Terrace	Step-round
Cathedral	Arch	Royal	Eliot
Connie	Victoria	Rutherford	Alton
Coverlet	Cozy Cover	Shaggy Tulip	Parrot Tulip
Daniel	Rickson	Silhouette	Taverne
Drape	Swathe	Simplicity	Classic
Five Band	Banded	Starlight	Tennyson
Floral Lattice	Flowerpot	Stonewall	Banner 'n Basket
General	Emperor	Sundial	Saf-Handle
Grape	Darwin	Target	Bullseye
Great American	Golden Key	Teardrop	Egg drop
Hercules	Aristocrat	Terrace	Step-down
Jerry	Monarch	Thick Rim	Big Lip
Medallion	Colonial	Viking	Bell
Murphy	Peel	Waverly	Crest
Norse	Everson	Wild Poppy	Poppy & Wheat
Novelty Radiance	Sunshine	Windcrest	Bronte
	Bulge	Yellow Rose	Pastel Rose
Perk	Deca-plain	Zephyr	Bingo
Pert	Sani-Grid		

Bibliography

Autumn Leaf News. National Autumn Leaf Collectors Club: Austin, TX.

Barth, Harold. *History of Columbiana County, Vol. II.* Historical Publishing Co.: Topeka-Indianapolis, 1926.

China and Glass Red Book. China and Glass Tablewares, Commoner Publishing Company: New York.

Cunningham, Jo. *The Autumn Leaf Story.* HAF-A Productions: Springfield, MA, 1977.

Cunningham, Jo. *The Collector's Encyclopedia of American Dinnerware.* Collector Books: Paducah, KY, 1982.

Duke, Harvey. *Superior Quality Hall China: A Guide For Collectors.* ELO Books: USA, 1977.

Duke, Harvey. *Hall 2.* ELO Books: USA, 1985.

"History of the Hall China Company, East Liverpool, Ohio." Ceramic Abstracts and the Bulletin of the American Ceramic Society. August 15, 1945.

Jewel Home Shopping Service Catalogs. Jewel Home Shopping Service: Barrington, IL.

The Jewel News. Jewel Tea Co., Inc. Barrington, IL.

Sears, Roebuck and Co. Catalogs. Sears, Roebuck and Co.: Chicago, IL.